THE BUFFALO NEWS

JOSH ALLEN
BUILT FOR
BUFFALO

This book is available in quantity at special discounts for your group or organization.
For further information, contact:

Triumph Books LLC
814 North Franklin Street
Chicago, Illinois 60610
Phone: (312) 337-0747
www.triumphbooks.com

Printed in U.S.A.
ISBN: 978-1-62937-991-3

The Buffalo News
Mike Connelly, Editor and Vice President
Margaret Kenny, Deputy Managing Editor
Josh Barnett, Executive Sports Editor

Content packaged by Mojo Media, Inc.
Joe Funk: Editor
Jason Hinman: Creative Director

Front and back cover photos by Harry Scull Jr./Buffalo News

Cover design: Jonathan Hahn

CONTENTS

INTRODUCTION

By Vic Carucci

At times, the search seemed hopeless. Quarterback after quarterback, season after season, and the result would always be the same.

He's no Jim Kelly. Don't even mention him in the same breath as the best the Buffalo Bills ever had behind center.

This went on for the better part of 24 years. Sure, there was that captivating stretch of Doug Flutie magic in 1999. There was that impressive half season that Drew Bledsoe had in 2002 before his career finally fizzled.

But there was nothing that came remotely close to resembling what the Bills had with Kelly. That explosive K-Gun, no-huddle offense that moved up and down the field like a fast-breaking basketball team, exhausting defenses and piling up points. That ability to dominate week after week. That sense that, with Kelly on the field, the Bills always had a chance.

Enter Josh Allen and the 2020 Bills.

His assault on the team's passing records while leading the Bills to a 13-3 record, their first AFC East championship since Kelly's Bills won it in 1995 and first appearance in the conference title game since Kelly's Bills got there in '93 put an official end to the search.

Allen arrived in 2018, as the seventh overall pick of the NFL draft, but his rookie season was more about providing promise than any definitive sense the Bills finally had their guy. In 2019, he made strides, but there still was more hope than relief.

Allen's 2020 season took care of that.

"They gave him the keys two years ago, but he didn't even put the keys in the car two years ago," Bills Hall of Fame receiver Andre Reed said. "This year, he started it up and actually drove it."

The 2020 season didn't end in the Super Bowl, as Kelly's Bills did four years in a row. However, Allen accomplished plenty that put him in the same neighborhood as Kelly and every other elite quarterback.

Start with the fact he finished second to Green Bay's iconic Aaron Rodgers, and ahead of Kansas City's iconic Patrick Mahomes, in NFL Most Valuable Player voting. Allen made that case by setting single-season franchise records for passing yards (4,544), touchdown passes (37), completions (396), 300-yard passing games (eight) and total yards (4,987, including 12 receiving).

"I think Josh loves the hype," offensive tackle Dion Dawkins said after Allen threw for 375 yards and four touchdowns to lead the Bills to victory against the San Francisco 49ers and their first Monday Night Football win since '99. "I think he loves to show people the truth. … Josh is one of those guys that's built for the big moments."

Unlike Kelly, Allen has much more than a great arm. He moves with far greater speed and elusiveness than his 6-foot-5, 237-pound frame would suggest.

"The less I see Josh Allen run, the better it is, but there are times where it makes it a lot harder on the defense when you have a quarterback to do what he does," Kelly said.

Allen also put to rest questions about his accuracy

Josh Allen meets with the media after practice at Buffalo Bills training camp at St. John Fisher College in August 2018. (Harry Scull Jr./ Buffalo News)

that lingered since his days at the University of Wyoming, where he completed 56.2% of his passes. In 2020, he had a career-high completion percentage of 69.2. His adjusted completion percentage – which accounts for spikes, throwaways and throws impacted by hits – climbed from 71.2 in 2019 to 79.2, according to Pro Football Focus.

The arrival of receiver Stefon Diggs in a trade with the Minnesota Vikings in March 2020 gave Allen a transformative target. Allen took full advantage, allowing Diggs to lead the league in receptions and receiving yards.

"He just keeps it in the simplest form for a receiver ... That just gives me confidence," Diggs said. "I can just play ball and my quarterback is going out there throwing darts."

At long last, the Bills found their next Jim Kelly. ■

ROAD TO BUFFALO

DEEP ROOTS

What Drives Josh Allen? Start with His California Hometown

By Tim Graham | May 20, 2018

In a place this small and so remote, folks handle multiple roles.

Seems that every third person you meet here — on top of their regular job — used to be the mayor, serves on the city council, sits on the school board, works for the volunteer fire department or coaches sports.

Brady Jenkins is among these trusted Firebaugh uber-stewards. He's head of security for the Firebaugh-Las Deltas Unified School District. He has been a city councilman for five years, was mayor and previously coached football, wrestling, track and swimming.

And wherever the University of Wyoming football team played the past couple of seasons, Jenkins' garage became an alternate community center.

Josh Allen's games have been must-see events for a couple of years in his isolated, Central Valley farming hometown. Wyoming, a fair team in a middling conference, wasn't commonly broadcast on national television.

"People would call around to see who had the game," Jenkins said, "and with all my sports packages, I could say, 'I got it!'

"They would be running down the street to my house. My garage was full. We would watch the entire game and hang around and talk about our guy."

The way people in Firebaugh gather around a single television to watch Allen calls to mind those old-time communal gatherings around a radio to hear the World Series or Joe Louis fight for the title.

There's an unspoken compact between Firebaugh and the Buffalo Bills' new quarterback.

Allen and his family have remained true to their home. Rather than transfer to a football program with more banners and the opportunity for a grander stage, Allen stuck and changed expectations for Firebaugh High.

"I have such strong family ties with this high school," Allen said at his parents' 2,000-acre ranch, where they grow cotton, wheat and cantaloupes. "I felt it was necessary for me to play here.

"I'd been here my whole life. There was no point in changing. We were going to work with what we got and find a way."

In extensive interviews with The Buffalo News over the past month, those who've raised, coached and taught Allen were unanimous in their insistence Allen simply was born with a constitution that's hard-wired to compete.

Where he grew up only added deeper layers.

Firebaugh intensifies the flame inside him. That defiance — a refusal to be patronized or abide big-timers — is a trait the town and its most famous resident share.

"The Central Valley does take things personally," said Rep. David Valadao, the U.S. Congressman who represents Firebaugh. "The Central Valley, as a whole, always feels ignored.

"We always feel the two population centers of the state, San Francisco and LA, take advantage and overlook us. It's hard to get their attention and get them to be supportive of policies that would benefit us."

Firebaugh, like much of California's 21st congressional district, is rural, poor, predominantly Hispanic and supremely reliant on the agriculture industry.

Signs at the town line state Firebaugh's population

Josh Allen stands in the cotton fields at his family's farm in California's Central Valley. (Harry Scull Jr./Buffalo News)

Josh Allen comes from a family about to enter its fourth generation of farming. (Harry Scull Jr./Buffalo News)

is 7,619. Wonderful Pistachios, TomaTek and Olam International have processing plants here, yet the nearest McDonald's is 11.2 miles away, a radius that equals 380 square miles devoid of golden arches.

The Firebaugh Chamber of Commerce was established in 2011. Its Facebook page hasn't been updated in four years; the phone number has been disconnected.

Allen's graduating class had 164 students. California Department of Education data showed he was one of 14 non-Hispanic students in his class. This year, 95.3 percent of the district's students from kindergarten through 12th grade are Hispanic.

While the demographics are unalike, Western New Yorkers can relate to the potential inferiority complex that comes with being looked down upon by metropolises with steep resources and enviable attractions.

How a person or a community addresses such situations often is what truly matters.

"When you watch him, especially live, you see a guy that plays with an edge, a chip," said Bills General Manager Brandon Beane, who last month traded up to draft Allen seventh overall. "He cares about his teammates. It's not just about him.

"When you do your research, what you see is the loyalty. That's one of the characteristics you look for. Those were all things in his makeup that remind me of the same things Buffalo is about."

Allen comes from a family about to enter its fourth generation of farming on each parent's side. In town, his mom, LaVonne Allen, ran the Farmer's Daughter restaurant for six years.

Back in Allen Ranch's air-conditioned office two weeks ago, Joel and Josh Allen had a father-son conversation about Firebaugh and how it jibes with their perceptions of Western New York.

Josh: "Firebaugh shaped me to be the person, the quarterback I am today."

Joel: "And it's helped keep you grounded, you know?"

Josh: "It seems like Buffalo. Buffalo is a place I could

The University of Wyoming was the only school to visit Josh Allen's hometown of Firebaugh, Calif., to recruit the quarterback. (Harry Scull Jr./ Buffalo News)

see myself living forever."

Yet Josh Allen's loyalty to Firebaugh curbed the likelihood he would reach a Division I college program, let alone the NFL.

Recruiters didn't take his size, stats or highlight tapes seriously. He didn't receive a single scholarship offer, not even to nearby Fresno State.

"Big-time college programs," Beane said, "aren't pulling guys out of Firebaugh."

Allen played a season for Reedley College's nondescript program, but he began the season as the backup and required a break or two to capture Wyoming's attention. He also grew a few inches and morphed into a prototype QB body.

Still, playing at Firebaugh High provided no launching pad and nearly squelched his dream.

"You bet it did," Home Based Realty owner Craig Knight said. He's also a two-time Firebaugh mayor (his father and grandfather were mayors, too) and a third-generation Firebaugh volunteer firefighter.

"You can be a great athlete in Firebaugh, but unless you get seen, you can fall by the wayside. He just wouldn't let that stop him, and this is home."

The village respects him that much more for it.

Product of his place

Valadao, the Congressman, described Firebaugh as being "a little bit of the Wild West" and "pretty far out in a wide-open area."

The closest metropolitan area is Fresno, about an hour away. Fresno Yosemite Airport doesn't provide a slew of appealing flight options. Only 18 percent of its traffic is commercial.

San Francisco is 150 miles away; Los Angeles, 240.

Firebaugh does have an exit off a particularly tedious stretch of Interstate 5, but you'd still need to drive 18 more miles to reach its two-stoplight downtown. Along the way, signs stapled to telephone poles advertise "owl boxes" and "10 avocados for $1" and "100 percent chicken manure."

"You've got to want to go to Firebaugh to get to Firebaugh," Wyoming offensive coordinator and quarterbacks coach Brent Vigen said, "but Josh is a product of that place."

Once Arvid Allen somehow made it here from Eldsberga, Sweden, nearly a century ago, Firebaugh's future would be impacted with each generation.

Allen's great-grandfather was 16 when he emigrated through Ellis Island in 1924, changing his surname from Erlandson. The nickname "Swede" didn't involve paperwork. The aspiring farmer went to Chicago and then to Arkansas, where he met his future wife, Buelah, in a strawberry patch.

They found their way to Firebaugh's fertile soil and became enmeshed in the community's fiber.

Few aside from entrepreneur Andrew Firebaugh himself have had greater influence here than the Allens.

A sign outside the Ledford Rodeo Grounds explains the outpost was founded in 1854 as Firebaugh's Ferry, named for his conveyance across the San Joaquin River during California's Gold Rush.

Two of Swede Allen's sons teamed up to start Allen Brothers Farming. Alfred went by "Buzz" because he always was "busy as a bee"; Arvid was known as "Dink" because he was "as cute as a little Dinky Doll."

Back then, Firebaugh residents had to travel to Dos Palos to attend high school. The town centers are about 15 miles apart, but the area is spread so wide some students could live a 30-mile drive from campus.

Buzz and Dink crusaded for Firebaugh to have its own high school and donated the land upon which the school was built. Buzz was the Firebaugh-Las Deltas Unified School District's first president and served 12 years on the board.

Firebaugh High's gymnasium is dedicated to Buzz. He died at the start of Josh's senior season, but Josh channeled his late grandpa's spirit whenever he could, touching the gymnasium plaque before each game and scrawling Buzz's initials on his cleats.

"I think about my dad in moments like this," said Buzz's daughter, Cindy Best. "I was sitting there at the NFL Draft, looking at my nephew and thinking, 'Wow, this kid is from Firebaugh.'

"My dad fought to get this school built. My dad would be so happy right now. He would be totally overwhelmed."

Best was in Firebaugh High's first graduating class of '78. She would help her father irrigate the crops and handled insect patrol, and she was the prom queen. Now she teaches the AVID college-readiness program and English-language development at her alma mater.

She witnessed every step of the school's growth. She marvels at massive construction taking place on campus after a $15 million bond was approved.

Community pride in the school is evident. Even with renovations ongoing, the Firebaugh-Las Deltas campus is impeccably maintained and landscaped.

"We know how to get dirty, probably know how to drive a tractor, probably drive a pickup," Best said of the average Firebaugh resident. "We help our neighbors. We appreciate hard work and those who work hard.

"Life is a little bit slow. So we're probably a little more sheltered, growing up in the country, but we have wholesome values."

Success is earned

The Firebaugh Harvest Festival in late July or early August is a pretty big deal.

Locals still call it the Cantaloupe Roundup, a long-ago phenomenon when Firebaugh's population would explode with workers who — before machinery rendered the process obsolete — picked, washed and packaged melons on the spot.

In 1959, actor Walter Brennan from "The Real McCoys" television show fired the ceremonial starting gun.

Outside his real estate office, Knight and Joel Allen surveyed all four directions at the intersection of 10th Street and P Street. They pointed out six, eight, 10 storefronts that in the '50s and '60s were taverns geared to quench the Cantaloupe Roundup's thirst. There was a cathouse, too.

Firebaugh is considerably sleepier these days.

"If you kick a can down the middle of the road or throw something out of your car, everybody in town knows about it," said Jenkins, the school security director. "The whole town is a neighborhood block-watch program. Everybody puts in."

Success is earned in Firebaugh, and Josh Allen has

personified that. In some places, soaring off toward magnificent horizons might be met with resentment from those left behind.

Allen, though, seems to draw universal admiration because he chose to do things the hard way in Firebaugh's name.

"Why isn't there anybody out there saying, 'I hope he fails'? Because he never created that atmosphere in this town," Firebaugh-Las Deltas superintendent Russell Freitas said.

Although his district is small, Allen is not Freitas' first brush with an elite athlete. In Easton, Calif., he was a Pop Warner coach of future Chicago Bears and Green Bay Packers linebacker Ron Cox and spent time around future big-league pitcher Matt Garza at Washington Union High.

Freitas cried four times while talking about Allen's character during a 15-minute interview.

"He was more than a student," Freitas said. He paused seven seconds to compose himself. "When people ask me about Josh, I tell them he's the real deal.

"You want your children to be around him and connected with him. You would want him to be your daughter's husband."

Examples of Allen's commitment to Firebaugh are abundant. One of the highlights the town still talks about was his final game against rival Dos Palos, a team Firebaugh never had beaten in football.

"And they reminded me of it all the time," Joel Allen said. "Right before Dos Palos would play Firebaugh they would say, 'Oh, that's going to be an easy win.'

"Right before Josh's last game against them, I heard, 'Firebaugh's going to get another beatdown!' I thought, 'Hmm, I don't think so.' "

Buzz Allen, a month shy of 75, died from cancer Sept. 17, 2013. It was Joel and LaVonne Allen's 25th wedding anniversary.

Firebaugh waited until its Oct. 18 game against Dos Palos to stage a Buzz Allen tribute. The school rededicated the gym and held a moment of silence for Josh's grandfather in Eagles Stadium.

Josh completed 21 of his 35 passes for 364 yards and four touchdowns and ran for another touchdown in a 52-28 victory.

"I'd been waiting a long time for that day," Joel Allen said. "Now we're the ones to beat."

Firebaugh beat Dos Palos the next year, too, and has won three of the past five meetings against the school from which Buzz Allen vacated out of community pride.

Firebaugh High principal Anthony Catalan gets passionate when discussing the way private schools frequently siphon the best and brightest student-athletes from public schools.

"We take it personally that it's not who we are," Catalan said recently in his office. "We kind of despise it. We feel it's unfair because we're a little school, a public school, and playing schools with recruits just isn't athletics in its truest sense.

"We feel that as a community. That's not who he is. Could Josh have gone to San Joaquin Memorial or De La Salle? Sure, but his goal was to build something here in Firebaugh with the kids around him."

Now Bills country

Not even the Bills' scouts have been to Firebaugh. Not Beane, not head coach Sean McDermott, not the Pegulas. Not yet, anyway.

Vigen has seen it only because he is Wyoming's offensive coordinator. Wyoming was the lone university to honestly recruit Allen and trekked there with head coach Craig Bohl to court its quarterback.

"The character that comes with that upbringing is there — working hard, being respected — those are things that he values," Vigen said of Allen. "He comes from a good background."

As Allen ventures to the NFL, his hometown won't be letting go.

Bills games will be easier to find on TV than Wyoming versus Gardner-Webb, and Jenkins still will host his garage parties for whomever wants to come over.

A couple weeks ago, LaVonne Allen dropped by the high school before meeting Joel at Firebaugh Restaurant — a Mexican joint Josh highly recommends — for lunch. Along the way, people continually approached her about hatching plans to fly to Buffalo for this game or that.

Across the street from Firebaugh Restaurant, from an upper-deck patio atop Knight's realty office, a Bills flag rippled in the breeze.

BORN FOR THIS

From Pop Warner to Bills, Playing QB Was 'Only Thing' Allen Ever Wanted to Do

By Tim Graham | May 22, 2018

Josh Allen, all of 9 years old, was a backup tailback and safety on his first Pop Warner team.

The idea of throwing passes someday for the Buffalo Bills was outlandish. He seemed to have trouble making the Dos Palos Broncos' roster.

Allen stood on the sideline and watched his Broncos get slaughtered in a scrimmage against the Los Banos Tigers. Then the starting tailback needed a potty break. Allen dashed onto the field.

"And here comes this kid," Los Banos offensive coordinator Tyrell Jenkins said, punctuating his words by smacking the back of his right hand into the palm of his left.

"He was just playing," *smack,* "like it was a 0-0 game," *smack,* "just hitting," *smack,* "and hitting," *smack,* "and hitting," *smack.*

On the Los Banos sideline, head coach Michael Tate, defensive coordinator Chauncey Lee and Jenkins whooped about Allen.

"He was a shorty," Jenkins said, "but you just saw the passion. We're saying, 'Man, this kid is losing by 50 points! He just won't quit! If we had 10 of him? We're winning the league championship!'

"We just happened to say all this near his father, who we didn't even know."

Allen's performance apparently wasn't enough for Dos Palos. His dad said the Dos Palos coaches after the game reaffirmed the bathroom-breaker would continue to start. Plus, they cut Josh's little brother.

Josh and Jason Allen still were in elementary school,

far from developing into athletes with legitimate pro aspirations. Jason often was more physically developed than Josh, by most accounts was the greater athlete and would go on to play college baseball.

Joel Allen suspected his sons were being punished by rivalry politics.

The Allens are from Firebaugh, a town without a Pop Warner team at the time. Kids from Firebaugh used to attend Dos Palos schools until Josh's grandfather, A.E. "Buzz" Allen, fought to establish the Firebaugh-Las Deltas Unified School District in the 1970s.

Joel Allen sensed Dos Palos' coaches were being malicious toward his family.

"When I told Josh they cut his brother, well, Josh was furious," Joel recalled. "Josh went up to the coach and said, 'If you don't take my brother, then you don't take me.' "

Josh Allen turned in his jersey. His father was proud, but now neither of his boys had a team.

Until Joel remembered overhearing those Los Banos coaches fawning over Josh's ferociousness in a scrimmage defeat.

"If Joel was 25 feet farther away from us that day," Jenkins said, "it probably would have been something we talked about for years to come, like, 'Hey, I wonder whatever happened to that kid?' He had heart."

They wouldn't need to guess. That kid became an intriguing quarterback prospect at the University of Wyoming, and Buffalo selected him seventh overall in last month's NFL Draft.

Allen's career unfolded in part because, two days

Josh Allen watches his sister Makenna play softball for Firebaugh High School at a 2018 game in Dos Palos, Calif. (Harry Scull Jr./ Buffalo News)

after the Allens refused to be put in their place, Joel wheeled his big pickup truck from Firebaugh to Los Banos — 45 minutes away, with Dos Palos in between — and through the chain-link gate at Loftin Stadium, much to the glee of Tate, Jenkins and Lee.

"You got *a lot* of kids like that who don't get chances, and they just give up," Tate said. "In life, you really don't know what's going to come your way. You just got to keep on pushing."

Perseverance has been a hallmark of Allen's football trajectory. He overcame snubs and backup roles throughout his Pop Warner, high school, junior college and university days.

But without those Los Banos coaches, who knows what the butterfly effect would have caused?

"They believed in him from Day One," said Allen's mom, LaVonne Allen. "They genuinely loved Josh, loved our family.

"Your first coaches teach you to like or dislike a sport. If you get a bad coach who berates or humiliates a kid, they can push them out. But they were so complimentary and such good coaches, from the heart."

Competitive from the cradle

The first word Cindy Best remembers hearing her nephew say, as he reached toward the sky, was "Touchdown!"

Not quite the first word, LaVonne replied, although Josh might have uttered only a couple of words earlier. "Ball" and then "football" were in his initial vocabulary, too.

Josh's parents quickly realized his early fascination with sports was not for entertainment purposes only. The allure included a hot competitive streak.

"I think he was 4 years old," Joel said. "He was playing T-ball, where the games always ended in a tie regardless of the score. It was fun, watching them run around the bases and trying to make a play.

"But Josh took it seriously. After one game, he said, 'Dad, we scored more runs than those guys! It wasn't a tie!' He threw the biggest fit."

The Allens never were fans of specialization. Parents risk burning out their children or missing other opportunities by forcing them to focus on a single sport or, in some cases, one particular position.

All four Allen children — Josh and Jason are sandwiched between sisters Nicala and Makenna in the pecking order — participated in multiple sports. If there

was a league or a school within driving distance, then the Allens tried it.

Josh gave karate, golf, flag football, soccer and even gymnastics a whirl. The back flips were with Jason because LaVonne got sick of trying to corral her hellions at the facility while Nicala practiced.

Josh also stuck with basketball and baseball through high school. He played first base and pitched, his fastball clocking at 92 mph.

"I still think I could play college baseball or college basketball somewhere," Josh said without a morsel of sarcasm. "Playing sports year-round kept my competitive edge up, allowed me to train different parts of my body, and feel it developed me as a full athlete."

All five quarterbacks drafted in the first round this year played at least two sports in high school.

Many sports, one love

Throughout all Josh's athletic endeavors, however, there was only one sport he wanted to mainline into his veins.

"Once I played quarterback," Josh said, "that's the only thing I've ever wanted to do."

That brings us back to Pop Warner.

When Josh arrived at Los Banos, he hadn't played any quarterback. The coaches fought over what position he would play. Tate and Lee were defense-oriented and fancied his fearlessness at safety.

"He was a gamer," Lee said. "Regardless of where we would have asked the kid to play, he would have done it."

Jenkins, the offensive coordinator, won out. Los Banos' incumbent quarterback had started for them the previous season, but there was something about Josh's charisma that couldn't be denied.

So Los Banos' coaches suffered the other parents' grumblings and gave Josh a chance to run the show.

"Josh took it like he was an NFL quarterback," Jenkins said. A stupefied smile crossed Jenkins' face at the memory. "Right after the game, he would be talking about the game plan for next week, telling me what his favorite pass plays and run plays were for the upcoming opponent.

"And you were talking to a *9-year-old kid*."

Jenkins soon discovered he had trouble staying a few steps ahead of Josh's obsessiveness. As a challenge, Jenkins created play scripts for the next game and quizzed Josh about, say, the sixth play and why it was designed to set up the eighth or 11th.

Josh Allen's parents, Joel and LaVonne, recognized their eldest son's competitive spirit early, enrolling him in karate, golf, flag football, soccer and gymnastics. (Harry Scull Jr./ Buffalo News)

Josh was a savant in his absorption of schemes.

Amid the usual chaos of a youth sideline, Jenkins sometimes had to wrangle players while Josh was on the field. Josh would gesture at his offensive coordinator to let him call the next play, and Jenkins was comfortable with it.

Josh made checks at the line of scrimmage, repositioned his linemen before the snap, put receivers in motion, called audibles.

"We wanted to push him and push him and push him," Jenkins said, "so that when his opportunity came for high school he wouldn't be scared of anything because he's faced it all.

"That's they way it is with all our athletes. We're not teaching you to be a Pop Warner star; we're teaching you to be a high school player."

All three of Josh's Pop Warner mentors coach at local high schools now.

Tate is Los Banos High's linebackers coach. Jenkins is head basketball coach at Pacheco High, where he also coaches junior varsity football and baseball. Lee is Pacheco's defensive coordinator and head baseball coach.

Those Pop Warner afternoons, though, sure were fun.

"You see the dreams and excitement when all the kids stare into our eyes and live on every word that we say," Lee said, "because we're gods to them. But we were still kids ourselves back then."

Lee shook his head as he reminisced. One moment stood out to him: At a postseason awards banquet, he remarked some grousing parents weren't fully appreciating Josh's abilities.

Parts of the room responded with laughter.

"Are these people blind to the fact this kid is a bona fide stud?" Lee thought. "All they cared about was how much their kid was playing.

"We always thought, 'This kid is special.' He had that drive that he was always going to succeed, and that it's not about him. It's for his team.

"And he was 9 years old." ∎

THE BEST OF THE BEST

From Wyoming to the Bills, Allen Aims to be Among the All-Time Greats

By Tim Graham | May 24, 2018

Few people have experienced Wyoming football like Jerry Hill has. He's from there, still lives there, played for the university and, at 78, still attends some games at War Memorial Stadium.

He was a Baltimore Colts fullback until 1970, winning a Super Bowl. Since he retired, only four players from the University of Wyoming logged more NFL games.

So when is the last time Hill remembers Wyoming football being as exciting as it was the past two years with Josh Allen at quarterback?

"Well," Hill replied, "I thought Jimmy Walden was pretty entertaining."

Walden was Wyoming's quarterback in 1958 and 1959.

That is the program-jolting panache Allen brought to the Wyoming Cowboys.

Allen didn't annihilate the school's record books; he played 27 games. Other quarterbacks whipped the ball around the Skyline and Western Athletic Conferences with abandon over three or four seasons, but no Wyoming quarterback has thrown an NFL pass.

The Buffalo Bills last month made Allen the highest Wyoming draft choice in NFL history.

Buffalo traded up to select him seventh overall, the latest in a sequence of overachieving moments that took Allen off the family farm in miniscule Firebaugh, Calif., through zero scholarship offers out of high school to modest Reedley College and a solitary Division I opening.

In itself, Wyoming's scholarship didn't guarantee much. Wyoming's lack of a track record was another challenge Allen had to conquer on his longshot odyssey.

"It was something I always wanted," Allen said at his One Bills Drive introductory news conference. "To say that I was sitting there, knowing it was going to happen, I couldn't say that. It was a long road, a long journey in front of me. It was very frustrating at times. But, in the end, I'm sitting here."

Although Wyoming has a reasonable NFL registry for a non-power conference that must recruit to a small town such as Laramie, the program's history provided zilch to forecast Allen's future.

"When you go out and do what he did in his career at Wyoming, yes, there were people who believed in him," Chicago Bears receiver and favorite Wyoming target Tanner Gentry said.

"But I guarantee there were more people who didn't."

Wyoming has boasted two all-conference quarterbacks, Paul Toscano in 1967 and Randy Welniak in 1988 and one national passing leader, Josh Wallwork in 1996. None was drafted.

The lone Wyoming products to have thrown an NFL pass are running backs Jim Kiick in the early 1970s and Jim Crawford in 1963.

Just one Wyoming player, former Bills guard Conrad Dobler, has started more than six NFL seasons. Allen's

Josh Allen poses for the press at New Era Field after being selected by the Buffalo Bills as the seventh overall pick in the 2018 NFL draft. (James P. McCoy/Buffalo News)

rookie contract will be four years with Buffalo's option to extend for a fifth season.

If Allen can channel in the NFL the same upstart spirit he displayed in Laramie, then perhaps he can accomplish a first for Buffalo — as he has for Firebaugh, Reedley and Wyoming.

"I want to be the quarterback that brings the Super Bowl to Buffalo," Allen said recently on his family's farm in Firebaugh. "With all the success that's happened there, it's never been done.

"I want to be that guy. To be talked about like Jim Kelly one day would be fantastic. To know I helped a city accomplish its dream of winning a Super Bowl — hopefully multiple — that's why I play the game.

"I want to be regarded as one of the best to ever play. To do that, you've got to win Super Bowls. And to solidify your legacy within a city, not many people can say that."

Sure supersedes being compared to Jimmy Walden.

A repetitive rah-rah talking point about Kelly was that he played quarterback with a linebacker's mentality.

Super Bowls or not, a quarterback who approaches the game like a special-teamer likely would go over well in Western New York.

"He's got that Steve Tasker, Bill Bates mentality, that work ethic where they gave it all they got," said Ernie Rodriguez, Allen's offensive coordinator at Reedley. "He just happens to be blessed with a frickin' rocket."

From Wentz he came

Wyoming offensive coordinator and quarterbacks coach Brent Vigen has held future NFL stardom in his hands.

Vigen came to Laramie with head coach Craig Bohl from Division I-AA North Dakota State, where their quarterback was Carson Wentz, another late physical bloomer with no big-school offers out of high school and who attended a university with no previous NFL-QB pedigree.

Wentz started two seasons at North Dakota State and proved tantalizing enough for the Philadelphia Eagles to draft second overall in 2016. He was enjoying an MVP-caliber season for the eventual Super Bowl champs until a left knee injury felled him.

Wentz measured 6-5 1/4 and 237 pounds with a 10-inch hand size at his NFL Scouting Combine two years ago. Allen checked in at 6-4 7/8, 237 pounds, 10 1/8 inches.

"Their physical comparisons are obvious, but the numbers are numbers," said Vigen, who recruited both. "They both have a great desire to compete at the highest level. They both go about their business the same way.

"Carson, obviously, has excelled to great heights in his first two years. Time will tell for Josh, but I certainly like the track that he's on."

Gentry spent 2017 working with last year's second overall draft choice, Chicago Bears quarterback Mitchell Trubisky.

Admittedly biased and with a brief glimpse of the NFL so far, Gentry insisted Allen has what it takes to excel at the next level.

"He can do whatever he wants," Gentry said. "He has every single tool you need to be the best quarterback in the league, and I know he won't stop until he gets there."

Gentry was a senior during as Allen's first full season as Wyoming's starter.

Allen led the Mountain West Conference in touchdown passes and total yards, helping the school notch its first victory over a ranked opponent since 2002 (and then did it again) plus go undefeated at home for the first time in 20 years.

Gentry caught 72 passes and led the Mountain West Conference with 1,326 yards and 14 touchdowns.

One touchdown in particular made Gentry laugh when asked to relay a quintessential Allen moment.

Allen threw for 334 yards and four touchdowns in a 69-66, triple-overtime loss to UNLV. Three of the strikes were to Gentry, the first came 64 seconds before halftime.

Allen delivered Vigen's play call to the rest of the offense, but then took Gentry aside for special instructions.

"He basically tells me to scratch what the play call was supposed to be and told me to run a go route," Gentry said.

Gentry bolted up the right seam. Allen nestled into the pocket and, from his own 46-yard line, threw a

Josh Allen participates in his first Buffalo Bills minicamp in May 2018. (Harry Scull Jr./ Buffalo News)

perfect pass to Gentry at the goal line. UNLV cornerback Darius Mouton had tight coverage as they leapt. Gentry snagged the ball with his right hand and pinned it to his armpit for the 48-yard touchdown.

"That's what I loved about him, the gunslinger mentality," Gentry said. "He wanted to make big plays and knew he could do it."

Allen decided after his strong 2016 season to enter the upcoming NFL Draft. He met in Firebaugh with agent Tom Condon of the powerful Creative Artists Agency and decided to make the leap.

Allen's decision didn't last until the next morning. He felt queasy about informing Bohl and Vigen. That alerted Allen he wasn't making the right choice.

The 2017 season at Wyoming wasn't as kind. The Cowboys lost four all-conference players, including Gentry, second-busiest target Jacob Hollister, Wyoming career rushing leader Brian Hill and center Chase Roullier.

Allen missed two games with a shoulder injury. His numbers plummeted as a passer (3,203 yards to 1,812 yards, 28 TDs to 16 TDs) and runner (523 yards to 204 yards, seven TDs to five TDs).

His total-offense average shrank from 266.1 yards to 183.3 yards a game.

"Last year, I think his problem was being gun shy," Hill said, "because the offensive line couldn't keep anybody out of the pocket, and he didn't have his receivers from the year before.

"I think Josh was overwhelmed, but if Buffalo can get him three or four seconds, he'll do really well."

Leaving Laramie

Allen had one season of NCAA eligibility left and could have returned to Wyoming for 2018.

But there's only so much a quarterback can accomplish in Laramie.

He signed with four CAA agents, including Condon and Todd France, whose personal firm was purchased by Bills owner Terry Pegula in 2011. When Pegula had to divest himself from the agent biz to purchase the club in 2014, France re-acquired his firm and eventually moved to CAA.

France also represents Bills quarterback AJ McCarron and former Bills quarterbacks EJ Manuel and Cardale Jones.

Condon represents quarterbacks Drew Brees, Matt Ryan, Eli Manning, Alex Smith, Matthew Stafford and Sam Bradford and handled Peyton Manning.

Last year's seventh overall draft choice, San Diego Chargers receiver Mike Williams, signed a fully guaranteed four-year, $19.75 million contract. Allen can expect that plus inflation, with an additional premium for being a quarterback.

Imagine how far that would go in Firebaugh or Laramie or Orchard Park.

Allen already has. He has been drooling over Southtowns real-estate listings online and how much house he can buy there.

Money, though, seems secondary to him and his family. Even with the hardships his parents have endured with agriculture the past seven years, Joel Allen scoffed at the thought his son's imminent wealth could save the family farm.

Before the draft, Allen Ranch was able to secure financing to stay afloat.

Josh Allen's business is all about football and, from the moment NFL Commissioner Roger Goodell called the quarterback's name, the enterprise is Buffalo.

"Tears were flowing everywhere at the draft because we all know what kind of kid he is, how hard he works, how polite and respectful he is," his uncle, Todd Allen, said. "He's the total package.

"I never dreamed anyone I know could throw it over 80 yards in the air. I just can't believe how it all turned out."

Now that Allen is in the NFL, he must reconcile being a team player with his desire to take over the Bills' offense, to deliver the same sort of entertainment he did with Wyoming the past two years.

He has needed to wait his turn at multiple steps along the way before getting his shot. A slower roll seems to have helped his development so far.

"He's not satisfied with just making a roster," Rodriguez said. "He wants to be The Man. That's the key."

McCarron is entering his fifth NFL season. He started four games for the Cincinnati Bengals, once in

Josh Allen felt an immediate affinity for Buffalo, noting similarities between Western New York and Firebaugh, Calif., where he grew up. (Harry Scull Jr./ Buffalo News)

the playoffs. Nathan Peterman returns to Buffalo after making two starts last year as a rookie.

Allen has been deferential but isn't bashful about his mission.

"They drafted me to play, drafted me to be their quarterback, hopefully, for the next 15-plus years," Allen said. "I'm not going to be pressuring myself — and I don't think I'll be pressured by my coaches — to get on the field right away.

"I have to learn behind AJ, learn behind Nate. I'm not expecting it to be pretty right away, but when I do get my shot, I'm going to make sure I'm prepared and trust my coaches and teammates."

Allen already has taken a shine to Western New

York. It fits with the small towns he has known.

A substantial difference — beyond the money — is that unlike Firebaugh or Reedley or Laramie, playing football in Buffalo provides an actual chance to win the championship.

What a heady thought. Whether this year or next, Allen expects to be one of the NFL's 32 starting quarterbacks alongside Aaron Rodgers, Cam Newton, Ben Roethlisberger, Russell Wilson.

The name that makes him savor the idea, though, is his favorite, New England Patriots legend Tom Brady.

"Now I get to play him twice a year," Allen said.

He stopped for moment, unable to stifle a grin.

"And beat him twice a year." ∎

POLARIZING PROSPECT

How the Bills' Front Office Arrived on Allen as the Team's Franchise QB

By Jay Skurski | July 19, 2018

After what they went through to go see him, perhaps it's fitting that the Buffalo Bills selected Wyoming's Josh Allen as their next franchise quarterback.

Thousands of hours of scouting went into the team's research. So, too, did one terrifying plane ride – which General Manager Brandon Beane recently recounted.

"There's video evidence somewhere, but we were coming in – we flew in private – and we were coming in over the mountains and the plane started just doing like this," Beane said, with his hand violently shaking. Assistant General Manager "Joe Schoen has video of it, but literally your head was going off the ceiling."

Team owner "Terry (Pegula) was standing by me – we were watching some video of Josh on our iPads – and we're going through some plays and progressions and things like that, and literally he is grabbing on to try to get back to his seat and we're bouncing around."

During a session with reporters last month, Beane said coach Sean McDermott stayed pretty calm. The same couldn't be said for offensive coordinator Brian Daboll.

"Daboll is FaceTiming his wife, and it was like Fred Sanford, 'I'm coming!'" the GM joked.

After the plane was safely on the ground, the pilots told Beane and Co. that they had gone through a "mountain wave," which forms when a strong wind blows across a mountain range.

"So then we Googled mountain wave and saw some bad history of mountain waves," Beane said. "I think after that we were a little distracted about how we were getting out of there. Like, where do we drive to have the plane meet us?"

The Bills' brain trust safely got home, returning with what promises to be a decision that will shape the future of the franchise.

"When we left Laramie, we felt really good about Josh," Beane said.

The process of landing on that conclusion started almost a year ago. Beane and Schoen spent much of last August reviewing the 2016 game film of the draft-eligible quarterbacks. That expanded beyond the four quarterbacks whom most analysts had as first-rounders: Allen, Oklahoma's Baker Mayfield, USC's Sam Darnold and UCLA's Josh Rosen.

"A lot of quarterbacks because at that point you're still trying to figure out who has what skill set," Beane said.

Even on tape, Allen's arm strength stood out.

"The next step was watching him through the year, and then going to see him play live," Beane said. "The great thing about seeing a guy play live at quarterback is yes, I can see all the stuff that I can watch on film, but I can see all the stuff in pregame.

"How's he interacting with his guys? When they're going through stretch lines, is he patting them on the

Josh Allen and fellow Buffalo first-round pick Tremaine Edmunds talk to the press after becoming part of the Bills organization in 2018. (James P. McCoy/Buffalo News)

butt and getting them going? When they go three-and-out two series in a row, what's he doing? When he comes off, who's he talking to? Is he talking to one guy? Is he screaming at people? Is he a mute? What's his leadership like? It's such an important part of playing that position because we all know you're going to have those days or weeks when you lose three in a row. How's he going to respond? Can he handle adversity?"

The next step was meeting with Allen at the Senior Bowl, where McDermott got a chance to see him throw live for the first time.

"We spent like 30 minutes with him … and we really found out how smart he was," Beane said. "He was nervous. You could see his nervousness the first time he met with us. I didn't think he was his true self from a personality standpoint. Daboll was killing him with questions, and you saw a guy that was really smart."

Allen was easily the most polarizing prospect in the draft. Opinions ranged from this – from CBS Sports' Pete Prisco: "They get the best QB in the draft and they had to go make the move to get him. Love the trade, love the pick" – to this, from Football Outsiders' Aaron Schatz: "I would rather have Tyrod Taylor quarterbacking my team over the next four years than Josh Allen." Heck, a producer for WGR 550 even followed through on a promise to quit if the Bills drafted Allen.

His completion percentage at Wyoming – 56 percent – fueled most of the negative scouting reports. Beane wasn't scared off, though. As part of the evaluation process, the Bills' general manager did more than just watch every one of Allen's throws multiple times. He also asked whether each of the other quarterbacks in the draft could have made them.

"He had no gimme throws," Beane said. "There's no, basically like handoffs, the bubbles and all that stuff. It was all a traditional pro style, throwing the ball vertically, and you basically have to do your own stats. How many times did he bail out of there and throw it away?"

As a result, the Bills came up with their own statistics on Allen and the rest of the quarterbacks. On the throws Allen did miss, Beane kept coming back to one thing.

"It was pretty clear it's when his feet were not right," he said. "The most positive thing I saw, when he was at

the Senior Bowl, his feet were in a much better position that week. He was much more accurate, not only during the week, but even in the game."

The other part of the Senior Bowl that Beane liked was Allen's competitive nature.

"I know his agents were all wanting him to play a series or two and get out because everyone is fearing injury – and he was like, 'No, I'm coming back in the second half,' " Beane said. "His agent was probably like, 'Why?' He came back and led them on two different touchdown drives."

Allen totaled 158 yards passing on 9 of 13 attempts and touchdown passes of 19 yards and 27 yards, but he was 2 of 5 in the first half for 14 yards and was sacked once.

During the Bills' private workout of Allen, Daboll had him make 42 different throws, without telling him beforehand what they would be.

"It's, 'OK, throw the deep dig now. Five-step, this. Go.' And he processed it quickly," Beane said. "Hey, it's Cover 2 – all that stuff, mental, physical. He didn't get to practice those throws. Yes, some of them he has done, but he didn't get to practice every throw that was coming. His footwork was very good, his workout was very good. We left there, we felt very confident."

Allen has said the Bills were his only private workout.

Just as he did before the draft, Allen has spent this summer refining his footwork with quarterbacks coach Jordan Palmer in California.

"He's going to work at it. He wants it," Beane said. "He's probably one of his harshest critics when he misses a throw or misses a read or whatever."

The Bills' evaluation of Allen went far beyond just numbers.

"There were games where his stats were bad," Beane admitted. "Go look at his stats for Colorado State (10 of 20 for 138 yards, no touchdowns and no interceptions). But if you watch that game, they're not winning that game without Josh Allen. He was running the ball. He was their leading rusher, obviously leading passer. … All the things that he brings beyond just standing back and throwing the ball."

As you would expect, the Bills are completely sold on Allen's leadership abilities. That was put to the test

Josh Allen may have been a divisive draft pick in the moment, but the Bills' extensive scouting and background research paid off in a big way with the franchise quarterback. (James P. McCoy/Buffalo News)

in a way they didn't expect, when tweets Allen either sent or retweeted years ago that included racist language surfaced on the night before the draft.

"We think we have all the hay in the barn and ready to go. Then this breaks, and the way Brandon handled it – you guys have gotten to know him – it didn't rattle us," McDermott said. "It shook us a little bit, but it didn't really rattle us."

Instead, Beane went to work. He contacted Allen's agency and said he needed a phone call on the day of the first round.

"Just to hear his version of what exactly happened, give us the timeline of this whole thing," the GM said. "You could hear the frustration in himself, the embarrassment, all those words. But he never made an excuse. He could have said, 'Hey, I was 14 or 15.' He

never said it. He just basically explained each situation, kids being kids, or quoting lyrics and stuff like that. I found him very honest."

The Bills' evaluation of Allen went all the way up to minutes before the start of the draft. As Allen was about to be interviewed on the red carpet, McDermott silenced the war room as everyone turned their attention to the television.

"We turned it up to listen to his interview because now we could see him and hear him at the same time and see how he was going to handle what he was asked," the coach said. "He got asked, I believe, by two different interviewers and he handled it just as well as he did over the phone."

The Bills were sold. Allen would be the pick – and the new face of the franchise. ∎

THE
ROOKIE
ARRIVES

ANSWERING THE CALL

No Alternative Now but for Bills to Start Allen

By Jason Wolf | September 9, 2018

Josh Allen picked up a first down on his fourth snap of the day, which is far more than you can say about the other guy.

The Buffalo Bills' rookie quarterback, the seventh overall pick in the draft, made his regular season debut with 11:22 remaining in the third quarter of the team's unprecedented embarrassment of a season opener, a 47-3 loss to the Baltimore Ravens on Sunday at M&T Bank Stadium, by far the ugliest opener in franchise history.

Buffalo trailed 40-0 at the time, and with Nathan Peterman as the starting quarterback, had failed to pick up a first down in the first half.

Factoring in penalties, the Bills' offense managed minus-7 net yards on his 10 possessions.

That literally is less than nothing.

Peterman's second interception of the day finally prompted the switch.

After Sunday's performance by the two quarterbacks, it's clear Allen should receive his first career start in next week's home opener against the Los Angeles Chargers. It's tough to justify the alternative.

"It's a situation where you're sitting there and watching the team do bad and then having to see your defense go on the field," Allen said. "It's situational football. If you can move the sticks one or two times and get the defense off the field, that's when teams do well."

Allen didn't perform much better behind the Bills' soup strainer of an offensive line, at least at first, going three-and-out and taking a sack on his initial possession.

But soon enough, he had the Bills on the move, and against the Ravens' starting defense, to boot, driving the team 46 yards in 12 plays and into position for its lone score.

"Really, I thought he made some decisive throws finding some tight windows," Bills coach Sean McDermott said about Allen. "He used his feet at times, as well. I thought he had pretty good command of the huddle and the offense at the line of scrimmage."

Allen began his second drive by moving the ball on his own, running for 11 and 14 yards on consecutive plays to cross midfield.

"The good thing is he can run," running back LeSean McCoy said, "so that adds another dimension to the offense."

Allen then hit Andre Holmes with a 14-yard pass on third-and-long.

He drove the Bills to the 3-yard line, in fact, but was unable to overcome a continuous comedy of errors.

Penalties, poor protection and dropped passes short-circuited the drive.

After McCoy powered his way to the 3, left tackle Dion Dawkins was flagged for unnecessary roughness, backing the Bills up to the 18. Left guard Vlad Ducasse was then called for a false start, making it second-and-goal from the 23.

The Bills were granted a reprieve when Brandon Carr was whistled for pass interference on Kelvin Benjamin, giving Buffalo first-and-goal from the 3.

But they continued moving in the wrong direction.

Allen made a poor read by choosing to keep the ball, rather than handing off to McCoy, and was sacked.

Benjamin dropped a rifled pass in the back of the end zone. And Allen was sacked again before the Bills

Josh Allen's regular season debut with the Bills was far from perfect but still a bright spot in an otherwise demoralizing loss to the Ravens. (James P. McCoy/Buffalo News)

settled for a 35-yard field goal from Stephen Hauschka.

It was a disappointing end to the team's most productive drive of the day.

But that field goal ended up being the only thing keeping this disaster from becoming the worst loss in franchise history, the 44-point margin of defeat surpassed only in the Bills' 56-10 loss to the New England Patriots in 2007.

"As a defense, you always want the shutout," Ravens linebacker Terrell Suggs said. "But he came in the game, and he did a good job moving the ball, made some plays with his feet. We've just got to do better executing, especially when it's a change at quarterback."

Allen finished 6 of 15 for 74 yards and a 56.0 passer rating but didn't commit a turnover and led a scoring drive, which is also far more than you can say about Peterman, who was 5 of 18 for 24 yards, two picks and produced a passer rating of 0.0.

"I love Josh," said Bills receiver Zay Jones, who led the team with three catches for 26 yards, all with Allen in the game. "He plays hard. He did some good things when he came in there in the second half. He came in there and gave us a little bit of a run, but we need to

focus more on the entire team – not just the quarterback – offensive line, running backs, wide receivers."

And that's true. The Bills' issues on offense run deep.

Allen even out-rushed McCoy, finishing with 26 yards on four carries.

"I was going in, just trying to make plays, trying to help this offense move the ball," Allen said. "We didn't put many points on the board. It's a tough game to start out with. Fortunate enough, in the NFL, this is one game. It's one loss. And you've got 15 more opportunities to go out there and play well."

In a roundabout way, McDermott said he'll consider starting Allen next week, though he wouldn't commit to anything other than reviewing the tape and all players at every position.

"I'm going to look at everything," he said. "It's too early to go one way or another. When I look at everything, I'm going to be objective and make sure we put ourselves in situations to win games."

There's undoubtedly plenty of blame to share, and much to fix.

Allen may not lead the Bills to a victory, but he offers the best chance to move the ball. ■

GAINING MOMENTUM

Allen Shows Why He 'Personifies Buffalo' in Triumphant Return

By Vic Carucci | November 26, 2018

The theme of the day was about toughness, about backing down from no one, about giving as good as you get. Heck, even Sean McDermott showed up for his postgame news conference Sunday with spots of blood on the front of his gray sweatshirt.

"Part of it's mine and part of it's probably a little bit from the scrum there," the coach said after the Buffalo Bills' 24-21 victory against the Jacksonville Jaguars. The "scrum," which came late in the third quarter, resulted in Bills defensive end Shaq Lawson and Jaguars running back Leonard Fournette being ejected. It also set the tone for a goal-line stand that ended with the Jaguars missing a field goal.

But the grittiness didn't end there or with the combined 23 penalties for 170 yards. As far as McDermott was concerned, the very essence of what the Bills showed in winning their second game in a row and beating a team that played in the AFC Championship game last January was their rookie quarterback, Josh Allen.

"I love his fire," McDermott said. "He personifies Buffalo, right? He's a hard-worker, blue-collar kid and loves to compete."

In case you were wondering what the Bills missed with Allen out of the lineup the last four games, the rookie returned from an injured throwing elbow in convincing fashion. His mostly solid performance wasn't about gaudy passing numbers; he completed only eight of 19 passes for 160 yards and a touchdown.

It was more about the way he stood tall in the pocket and took hits. And it was about the way he ran: 13 times for a Bills quarterback record 99 yards and a score.

"My expectations were that I'd be back, I'd be better mentally and, obviously, physically with the elbow holding up, and I just wanted to go out there and complete the ball when it needed to be completed and make plays when plays needed to be made," Allen said. "I trust the guys around me, and that's kind of what we did today."

The impressive athleticism and physicality that were a large part of why the Bills made him the seventh overall pick of the draft were evident on a 14-yard touchdown run for a 21-14 lead they would never relinquish early in the third quarter. Allen also had a 45-yard sprint with under seven minutes left.

Offensive coordinator Brian Daboll loaded the game plan with runs to take advantage of the Jaguars' man-to-man coverage, with defenders often playing with their back to the quarterback.

"I mean, they went split safety quite a bit," Allen said. "And their 'Mike' (middle linebacker) was really a (third safety), especially when we did go empty (set), so that opens up a lot of lanes for the quarterback to run."

Josh Allen rushes for a touchdown over Jacksonville Jaguars defensive end Yannick Ngakoue (91) in the fourth quarter of the 24-21 Buffalo win. (James P. McCoy/Buffalo News)

The runs would have been the highlight of Allen's day had he not delivered a couple of important throws that allowed the Bills to take a 14-0 lead in the first quarter.

The first was a 32-yard connection with Kelvin Benjamin. Cornerback Jalen Ramsey – who had called Allen "trash" in the August edition of GQ magazine and stood by his critical remarks about the Bills making him the seventh overall pick in the draft in a tweet earlier in the week – picked up a facemask penalty on Benjamin that added 15 yards. After an 11-yard Allen pass to Jason Croom, Isaiah McKenzie sprinted six yards into the end zone.

The second impressive play from Allen's throwing arm was a 75-yard touchdown pass to Robert Foster. It was the longest scoring throw by a Bills rookie and the team's longest pass completion since Tyrod Taylor connected with Marquise Goodwin in 2016. Making it even more remarkable was the fact defensive linemen Dawuane Smoot and Yannick Ngakuoue simultaneously crashed into Allen as he released the ball, preventing him from seeing the score.

"We had Zay (Jones) on basically a curl route about 18 yards down the field, so I felt like the corner kind of jumped it," Allen said. "Robert saw the safety deep, cut in front of his face, and I didn't even really see it get caught."

The first trait that LeSean McCoy liked about Allen from the first time they met was his attitude.

"He wants to win," the running back said. "He's no chump. He plays hard. They talked about him, so he couldn't wait to get out there and prove them wrong."

"Josh's return was great, definitely what we needed," Jones said. "I know there was a lot of questions of, 'Are we going to keep this momentum going?' and things like that from two weeks ago, and Josh did a great job of coming in, using his legs for plays, extending plays, hitting Robert Foster with a beautiful ball down the field."

During a crazy sequence late in the third quarter, the Jaguars went from what was initially ruled a touchdown catch by Donte Moncrief to a first down at the Buffalo 1 to being backed up by penalties and ultimately missing a 42-yard field goal.

Along the way, they lost their best offensive player, Fournette, who sprinted from the Jaguars' bench to start brawling with Bills players in the northwest corner of the field.

"You just can't say enough about how we kind of pulled together here," Allen said. "It's an exciting win and it's definitely, hopefully, going to carry some momentum into next week."

The larger question, of course, is the extent to which Allen's performance follows him into Sunday's game at Miami and beyond.

"He's still young, so again, let's manage expectations," McDermott said. "It was a good start for him. These (final) six games ... (are) to get him back on the field and grow and see different defenses. ... (Jacksonville is) a team that likes to get in your face and play a physical brand of football, and so do we."

Just check out the blood on the coach's sweatshirt. ∎

Josh Allen celebrates with fans after the win over the Jaguars in his return from injury. (Harry Scull Jr./Buffalo News)

'A CLASS ACT'

How Allen Formed a Special Bond with Fans

By Jay Skurski | December 22, 2018

If I ever make it big one day, Josh Allen thought to himself, I'm not going to act like that guy.

Growing up in Firebaugh, Calif., the Buffalo Bills' rookie quarterback was a big San Francisco Giants fan. He recalled this week a moment that has shaped his approach ever since.

"I won't mention his name, but there was a pitcher for the Giants. He had a fantastic game and we were all excited," Allen said. "We went down to the tunnel. There were maybe 15, 20 kids there — not a huge amount — and he came out of the locker room after he had changed. He was the last one to leave. We were all waiting there. He turned his head and walked straight the opposite direction. Didn't wave, didn't look, didn't say thank you. As a kid, I could never root for a guy like that again.

"I told myself if I got to be in this position, I'd go out of my way to do small things like that."

Allen has lived up to his word in his first professional season. It was common to see him signing autographs after every practice of training camp for at least 45 minutes.

"I was that kid before," Allen said. "I was in the same spot. I was looking up to guys, wanting to meet them and get to talk to them. I told myself if I ever got the opportunity to be in the NFL, I'd make sure that I would do the right things. If there was any kid that wanted to talk or have me sign something, that I was going to go out of my way to try and do that."

Allen's generosity particularly left an impression on Jordan Peterson, a 16-year-old from North Dakota who is a double lung transplant recipient and a huge Bills fan. That's been passed down from his parents, Dan and Annette, both of whom grew up in Western New York — Dan graduated from Niagara Wheatfield and Annette from North Tonawanda.

"Her parents had original season tickets to the Buffalo Bills back in 1960 at the Rockpile," Dan said of his wife. "So our families have been Bills fans our entire lives."

A job opportunity took Dan to Fargo, N.D., in 1998.

"So we've been here the last 20 years, voices in the wilderness," Dan said. "My boys have inherited that love of the Bills. They sit next to me on Sundays, and it's been a big part of our family."

Suffering from cystic fibrosis, Jordan received a double lung transplant in 2011.

"When we got the news, it was so overwhelming, when they gave us all the statistics. At the time, for children with a lung transplant the five-year survival rate was — I remember distinctly them telling us — 38 percent," Dan said. "So, my wife and I, it was a sobering day when we walked out of the hospital. We sat in the car, I can remember just being overwhelmed at the enormity of everything that we were hearing.

"And Jordan said, 'Dad, what's wrong?' I said, 'Well, we have a lot to think about. A lot to pray about.' And he said, 'We have to do this. This is my only chance to have any life. There's nothing to think about, we have to do this.' That was just his attitude about life."

Jordan received his transplant on June 18, 2013. His first question to doctors after surgery was "Can I play sports again?"

At first, the answer was only noncontact sports. With no checking in squirts, that meant he could get back to playing hockey. As he kept going back for quarterly

Josh Allen signs autographs after practice on the first day of training camp in 2018 at St. John Fisher College. (James P. McCoy/Buffalo News)

checkups, Jordan continued to ask the same question, "Can I play football?"

Finally, after two years of hearing no for an answer, doctors responded, "We'll see."

"He walked out of the room and Jordan looked at me and said, 'He didn't say no, dad. I think there's a chance,'" Dan said. "They went back to the surgeons and said, 'Is there any reason why he can't play?' And they said, 'Well, not structurally.' His sternum had been wired back together and was healed, so he didn't have any higher risk of an injury that way. So he got permission and started playing sixth-grade football. So that's been a big thrill. He's our little 'Rudy' if you will."

After he returned to Fargo following his surgery, Jordan was given a grand welcome at Oak Grove Elementary. North Dakota State football coach Craig Bohl praised Jordan at a school assembly, calling him a "true hero."

When he appeared in two varsity games last season for Oak Grove Lutheran High School, the family believes Jordan became the first double lung transplant recipient in the country to play varsity high school football.

Bills General Manager Brandon Beane heard of Jordan's story through a mutual acquaintance he shares with Dan. That led Beane to invite the family to the game against Minnesota. They had front-row seats on the 50-yard line, providing an excellent view of Allen's now-famous hurdle of Vikings linebacker Anthony Barr.

"We all kind of stood up. My dad and I looked at each other like, 'Did that just happen?' It was incredible," Jordan said. "I hope he never does it again, though."

"He did tell me that," Allen said with a laugh.

The next time Allen saw Jordan, who made a visit to the Bills' facility in November, his cellphone case had "The Hurdle" on it.

"That was kind of cool," Allen said. "Being in this position where I am, kids are looking up to me, it's extremely surreal. To be in this situation and to use our platform for good, it makes it all worthwhile."

The Bills rolled out the red carpet for Jordan during his visit. Offensive coordinator Brian Daboll let him call a few plays during practice. Coach Sean McDermott had his arm around Jordan as he addressed the team at the end of practice. The message was about overcoming adversity, pointing to Jordan as an example. After McDermott's talk, Jordan broke down the team huddle.

"Micah Hyde came up to me and gave me a hug and we talked for a little bit. Coach McDermott was super nice," Jordan said. "Zay Jones came up and gave me his gloves. Jordan Poyer gave me his cleats. Josh gave me his game cleats. Harry Phillips gave me his gloves. Mr. Pegula, he was super kind. Brandon Beane was super kind. Tre White, I met him and he's a character. He was super nice to me."

"We just can't thank the Bills enough. It was such an awesome experience," Dan said. "Josh is just an incredible young man."

The Peterson family had been fans of Allen dating back to his time at Wyoming, where he played for Bohl. Meeting him only reinforced that.

"He was extremely kind," Jordan said. "He's a class act, I would say."

During Jordan's visit, he even pulled off a "Madden" video game victory over Allen.

"It was 21-20," he said. "He had a chance to win but he choked. He kind of tripped on the 1-yard line I guess and then my defense stopped him. But he won on Sunday so that was the important thing."

Reminded of the outcome, Allen largely declined comment.

"I don't want to talk about it," he said. "He exploited me on a few plays, and I won't go into any further detail. The results were inconclusive, I still think. That's what we're saying."

"Just to know that a type of kid like that is following me, it definitely puts things in perspective," Allen said. "Being on this level, you can use your platform for a lot of good. Just to see his face brighten up, it was awesome. He thoroughly enjoyed his time out here, and I'm just glad I got to be a part of it." ∎

Josh Allen, seen here with Bills super fan Pancho VillaBilla, makes it a point to spend time with fans and connect to the Buffalo community. (James P. McCoy/Buffalo News)

'WHEN IT'S FOOTBALL TIME, IT'S FOOTBALL TIME'

Allen on Rookie Season, Off-Field Life, Boyhood Heroes

By Vic Carucci | December 26, 2018

As a quarterback for a 5-10 team, Josh Allen has experienced more lows than highs since the Buffalo Bills made him the seventh overall pick of the NFL Draft in April.

The worst part was having to miss four games with a sprained elbow suffered in an Oct. 14 loss at Houston. Although it gave Allen a chance to step back and learn from watching others – mainly veterans Derek Anderson and Matt Barkley – prepare and play, he felt he was finding his groove against the Texans and wonders what might have been had he not been injured.

The 22-year-old Allen spent some time with The Buffalo News reflecting on a rookie season that ends after Sunday's game against the Miami Dolphins. He addressed a wide range of topics, including life off the field, his boyhood football heroes, relationships with offensive coordinator Brian Daboll, fellow quarterbacks Barkley and Anderson, and some of his other older teammates who he had contemplated giving walkers and canes as gag gifts for Christmas.

Buffalo News: With the high-profile nature of your job often pulling you in different directions, do you ever wonder if your life is your own?

Josh Allen: My life's my own. I've got a good group around me, most notably of my family, who I surround myself with. My agents and my marketing people do a really good job of kind of planning everything. When we do have appearances or events to go to, we try to line those up as close as they can (be to each other) and especially try to (schedule) things during the offseason. That's kind of my time when I can go do that.

During the season, it's really football and that's about it. I've told my agents and my marketing people, "When it's football time, it's football time. I don't really want to be messing with anything else." Obviously, there's some things that pop up that you have to do, but it's nothing too bad.

BN: How has your family adjusted to you being an NFL quarterback?

JA: They've adjusted well. They've been to almost every single home game. They love everything about Buffalo. The community kind of reminded us of Wyoming when I first got there. Because Wyoming is the only four-year institution in the state, so Laramie and everything around it is just all Wyoming Cowboys. And that's kind of the sense that we get here, it's all about the Buffalo Bills. And that's really cool.

BN: Who helps keep you grounded?

JA: Family, friends, girlfriend. Just the dynamics of how

The life of a rookie quarterback is never easy in the NFL, as Josh Allen learned well during the 2018 season. (Harry Scull Jr./Buffalo News)

I grew up. That's kind of what really keeps me grounded, where I'm from, my community that I go back to in the offseason, Firebaugh, Calif.

I'm just like anybody else. I love hanging out with the family, watching movies, playing video games. Just a normal person.

BN: What has been your favorite part about being an NFL quarterback?

JA: The platform it gives you, you get to do a lot of good. But being an NFL quarterback, it's the only thing I've ever wanted to be. Just being able to play football at the highest level, in front of some of the most amazing fans here in Buffalo — I think they're the most amazing fans that the league has — but just to be in a city, to be a part of a community and to be playing for an historic franchise.

BN: Is there a worst part?

JA: I don't think so. I mean, I think everybody that is notable or gets noticed when they go out and when I'm out to eat with my family or girlfriend or whatever the case may be, sometimes you get people who'll come over your table while you're eating. That's the hard part for me because I'm from a small community and everybody knows everybody. That's probably the only hard part and it's super minor. But there's no privacy, for lack of a better word.

But when there's kids, obviously, if I'm out, I want to take pictures and sign autographs for the kids because I was in their shoes at one point. There was a pitcher for the San Francisco Giants. I went through the tunnel where they went from the dugout to the clubhouse, and one of the players had one of their best games in their career. There were maybe 20 kids waiting out in the hallway before him, and he comes out, doesn't even look at us, turns his head and bee lines it out.

It didn't break my heart, but I was just like, "Geez, can't even wave?" So I always make sure to wave, high-five, look, whatever the case may be, just to let them know that I recognize them, that they're there (when) I may have something else to do and I can't sign or take a picture.

BN: How old were you then?

JA: I was maybe 10-11.

BN: Who was the pitcher?

JA: I'll keep him unnamed.

BN: You mentioned going to see the San Francisco Giants. What kind of a football fan were you?

JA: I grew up a Niner fan. I was on the West Coast, I loved the California quarterbacks — Tom Brady, Aaron Rodgers, obviously whoever was in San Francisco at that time. I just loved the game of football. I remember going to church and just begging my dad, "Let's hurry up and get home so we can watch the 10 o'clock kickoff." I really wasn't fully focused on one person as much as I was the entire game.

BN: OK, but of the players you watched growing up, someone had to inspire you the most to want to be an NFL quarterback, right? Who made you say, "I want to be that guy?"

JA: Brett Favre and Tom Brady. That's who I wanted to be.

BN: What did you like the most about those guys?

JA: With Brett Favre, just the way he played, the amount of fun he had. Dude never missed any games. Any time the Packers' games were on, he was playing. He was never out of a game, so you got to see him every given week. And then, obviously, Tom Brady with the success that he had at that time period when I was a young kid, loving the game of football, getting to see what he was doing.

When Brett Favre left and he went to Minnesota? That killed me for a while. I was like, "I can't be a fan anymore." I couldn't believe he did that. I understand why he did it now, but at the time, I was pretty disappointed. Still, that's the one guy who I wanted to be. He was just kind of an outgoing person. His teammates seemed to love him. His coaches seemed to love him.

He was never really disappointed. Obviously, you're going to be disappointed with games, but talking to the media and stuff, he was never down and out. He always

Josh Allen stood tall during a challenging rookie campaign, which paid off as he developed as a quarterback and broke through in subsequent seasons. (Harry Scull Jr./Buffalo News)

thought he had a chance. That's really what I loved most about him.

BN: What else, besides his success and California roots, drew you to Brady?

JA: He's very performance-based. His life revolves around the game of football. And that's where I looked at him and I was like, "I want to be like that." At the same time, I want to put my own flair on it. I want to be a fun guy who loves playing the game of football and everybody enjoys playing with me.

BN: What's the greatest learning experience you've had so far?

JA: After the Houston game, when I got to sit — or stand — and watch Derek and Matt. They showed me what it was like to be a professional football player, a professional quarterback — to come in, do things the right way, how they watched film, how they prepared for games, how they approached walk-throughs at practice and then how they prepared on game day, something that I hadn't seen before. They've been in the league for a combined 16-17 years, so they have a lot of experience. For me to see that, that was huge.

BN: How soon after suffering that elbow injury against the Texans did you realize you were going to be shut down for awhile?

JA: When I went off to the sideline. I tried to throw the next play and it didn't work out for me. That pain ... every thrower will tell you pain in the elbow sucks. It's the worst type of feeling, mentally, that you can have. It sucked, too, because that Houston game, I kind of started feeling things were slowing down. I was seeing things a little better, making better decisions and then the injury happens and I get to sit out for a while and learn from Matt and learn from Derek. I'm continuing to learn from them and it's still an ongoing process.

BN: How long did it take you to get over the disappointment and frustration of knowing you were going to be out of action?

JA: It was good a day after it. I was like, "Alright, I'm going to sit back. I don't expect to be out for more than a game." We were playing the Patriots on Monday night in two weeks, so I was like, "I'm going to be back for that game." I kept telling myself that.

As the game got closer and closer, I was like, "I'm really going to miss this game. It is what it is. I get to play the Patriots two times a year for, hopefully, the rest of my career. So I kind of put that in the back of my mind, let it go and I was good until I got back on the field and was able to show what I had learned.

BN: At 22, how hard is it to wrap your mind around the fact that you've got a teammate, Lorenzo Alexander, with a daughter who is almost your age?

JA: It's weird. We go over there for Bible study every other Thursday, and his daughter, Vanessa, was there (last week). And it's kind of mind boggling just knowing I'm closer in age to his kids than I am to him. It's kind of funny. I give him a few jabs about it.

BN: What kind of jabs?

JA: Every old-man joke you can think of.

BN: How amazed are you by Lorenzo's performance at age 35?

JA: He's playing at an extremely high level. For him to do what he's doing ... the trajectory of his career has been up and down and sideways, 360, whatever you want to say. He's seen it all, position changes.

You look at a professional football player, he's the epitome of it. How he handles himself, the things he does for the community, his foundation, how he is with his family, how good of a dad he is. That's one guy you can look at and say, "I can model myself after him and I'd be perfect in life." I mean, he's just one of those guys you look at (in) amazement, just the things that he does and continues to do are pretty spectacular.

BN: Is it at all awkward to being as young as you are and taking on the natural leadership role that goes with your position?

JA: I don't think so. I don't feel it, at least. You know, we're all teammates. How long you've been in the league,

Josh Allen grew up idolizing some of the best quarterbacks in league history, including Tom Brady, Aaron Rodgers and Brett Favre. (Harry Scull Jr./Buffalo News)

I don't think that really matters. We've got one common goal and that's to win football games and however I can help to win football games is what I'm going to do. I think everybody kind of respects that and they see the type of person I am, how I play the game. I play with a lot of passion and I think that the guys really enjoy that.

BN: Have you ever had to assert yourself just to remind everyone else in the huddle that you're in charge?

JA: No. For the most part we understand when I get in the huddle, when any quarterback gets in the huddle, it's the quarterback's time to talk. But I'm not the guy that's (swearing at) people or putting people down. I'm like, "Let's go do this. Let's go get this job done."

BN: Questions about your accuracy have followed you from college and are still a major part of the conversation about you. What's your take on it?

JA: Obviously, I mean, I want to complete the ball every time I step back and throw it, and that's just not possible. There's a lot of different things that go into completion percentage and what people want to see. There's throwaways, there's decision-making, there's drops, there's how far you push the ball downfield, types of throws that you made.

And I don't think (completion percentage is) the best metric to gauge accuracy. I really don't think that plays a huge part into how a quarterback should be evaluated. But at same time, I want to complete the ball at a higher rate, I do. I want to put the ball in our playmakers' hands and let them make plays.

BN: Is it fair to say that the specific work you did on your throwing mechanics before the draft with your quarterback guru, Jordan Palmer, and the work you did early on with the Bills' coaches has dissipated during the season and you'll pick it up again in the offseason?

JA: Yeah, yeah. There's always something to improve on. I'll be taking a little time after the season, let the body kind of recover, and then in February I'll get back to it, working on the fundamentals of just throwing and getting back to getting your arm loosened and start to make a schedule and a regimen and kind of living by it.

BN: What's your relationship like with Brian Daboll?

JA: Love him. I mean, he's awesome. Just the knowledge that he brings to the game. We're extremely close. He's not a coach you can't talk to. I can talk to him about anything, football, non-football. He cares about his players and cares about the quarterback room. I have a lot respect and a lot of love for Dabes. I think he's doing a terrific job.

BN: How about your relationships with Barkley and Anderson?

JA: We've had a really good relationship. It's a really good quarterback room. We know the task at hand. That's a room that just wants to win football games. They're helping me out. I owe a lot of credit to them, how they've helped me already and and how they're going to continue to help.

BN: What's a specific example of how you've been helped?

JA: Just the presence when we watch film, Derek seeing different looks than I have. He'll kind of tell me, "If they're an 'over' team and that three tech's misplaced, they're bringing pressure here." Just certain situations like that in film (study), where he just gives me kind of like these tidbits that I'm like, "I didn't even know that." I'm still learning the game of football, and they're still helping me. ■

The lessons of Josh Allen's rookie season helped lay the foundation for what could be an all-time great career with the Bills. (James P. McCoy/Buffalo News)

FACING
EXPECTATIONS

ALL EYES ON ALLEN

Quarterback Keeps Working Toward That 'Face of the Franchise' Expectation

By Vic Carucci | September 4, 2019

St. Joseph School in Firebaugh, Calif., was still a 15-minute drive away, but Josh Allen's education had already begun as he sat in the front passenger seat of his father's Chevy Silverado. Beginning at age 6 and for at least a couple of years thereafter, Josh could count on the "Interview." It was Joel Allen's way of preparing his son for the fulfillment of those lofty dreams of becoming an NFL quarterback.

Joel understood that being blessed with great physical talent would never be enough alone to make this to happen. His goal was to make sure Josh understood that as well.

As their early morning journey took them along Jerrold Avenue to Bullard Avenue to Highway 33, Joel would keep his left hand on the wheel while extending his right hand as if holding a microphone in front of Josh.

"Literally, every day, he'd sit there and ask me questions," Josh said. "He'd create a fake scenario about a game. 'How'd you feel out there?' My dad is very good at ad-libbing and a good BS-er.

"Looking back, he was just prepping me for, hopefully, one day what I could be."

This is what Josh Allen is at 23: a second-year starter for the Buffalo Bills. He represents more in the way of hope – attached to being a seventh overall draft pick – than accomplishment, although there were plenty of promising flashes from his 11 starts as a rookie in 2018. This season is all about what's next for the former Wyoming standout.

Will he be what the Bills have desperately sought since Jim Kelly threw his last pass for them when Allen was 7 months old? Will he become the face of the franchise?

It has long been a familiar theme throughout the NFL.

"I think every team is looking for that answer," Denver Broncos General Manager and Hall of Fame quarterback John Elway said. "That answer is hard to find. It's hard to be able to evaluate the heart and how they're going to handle the whole situation and the pressure of what it takes to be a quarterback."

Allen's development first will be measured in numbers, both his individual statistics and the team's won-loss record. Equally important, however, is the way he conducts himself.

"Generally, if you have a franchise quarterback, he's the face of your team," Bills General Manager Brandon Beane said. "Drew Brees, Aaron Rodgers, Tom Brady. So, what do you want representing your team? You want a guy who's a natural leader. You can try and train people all day long to be leaders, but there's only so much you can move the needle.

"You've got to have a guy that can not only get himself prepared and do the right thing, but also understands it can't be a sometime thing with a

As a child, Josh Allen prepared for the physical rigors of football as well as the leadership qualities necessary in a star quarterback. (Harry Scull Jr./Buffalo News)

quarterback. Everybody's watching him. Everybody in the building, not just the players. The equipment guys, the video guys. There's an energy off of that. If you have that guy, you know every Sunday you have a chance. You're going to win because of that guy, not in spite of."

Joel Allen's purpose with the daily interview ritual wasn't to provide his son with early media training. It was to help Josh to grasp the most critical element of fulfilling football's highest-profile position, which is to always be more accountable than everyone else on the team.

"One thing that he kind of taught me was, 'In victory, spread; in loss, take,'" Josh said. "So when things are bad – obviously, some guys may or may not do it – but putting most of the weight on your shoulders and just things that you could have done better to help the team. That's how I'll always be. If we don't have a good game, I take that very hard on myself, because there's things that I probably could have done better and probably I should have done better.

"I know, as a quarterback, that people look up to that position. They look at the body language. They look at how you talk, how you look, so trying to stay in that even mindset in the good and in the bad. Just how you talk to the media. I think how you portray yourself and putting the team above you and showing what the team needs and expects and not what you need or what you expect. I think that just goes hand in hand.

"The face of a franchise needs to be able to kind of relate to the media and be able to portray the message that he wants to for the better sake of the team."

Kelly echoes that sentiment. The Hall of Famer vividly remembers that grasping the concept of sharing and accepting blame, rather than dispensing it, didn't come naturally to him.

But he came to realize it was essential for a franchise QB.

"Early on, I had to learn that, because as a quarterback, you're a leader and you lead by example," Kelly said. "You have to learn that sometimes you keep things in. It's not what you say to a receiver; it's how you say it. If a receiver runs a route that wasn't quite the way it should have been, tell him what you were looking at rather than what he did wrong.

"Early on, I got frustrated with a couple of receivers and I think, more than anything, I learned how to tell them what I was seeing so that they knew it, too. You don't tell them how to do it, but why you think it should be done this way."

To Allen, no one better exemplifies what it means to fill those face-of-the-franchise shoes than the quarterback and fellow northern Californian he has admired since childhood.

"As much as I hate to say it, it's Tom," he said with a sheepish grin.

Allen knew very well his comment would offend a fan base that feels contempt for Brady and his team, the New England Patriots. Allen is all about having as strong a connection as possible with "Bills Mafia," a term he frequently uses and demonstrated as much during this summer's training camp at St. John Fisher College by consistently being the last player out signing autographs, especially for kids.

"But you've got to respect the guy," Allen said of Brady. "I grew up loving him and what he did on the field and how he was off the field. Just the way he carries himself, the way that people regard him, the respect that his teammates give him when they're not there, the way they talk about him when they're on a different team. I think everybody in the league can look at him and wish for that sustained success that they've had for so long.

"Every year, year in year out, he's still doing the right things. Looking at the little things like him never walking on the football field when he goes out to practice. As soon as he steps between lines, he starts jogging. Just little things like that that not many people pick up on, but I kind of look at. I'm not saying that I want to be Tom Brady, but as a young kid, I looked up to him like he is the role model. He is the Mecca. He is what you would strive to be as a quarterback."

For Allen, doing the right things included spending parts of February through April working in Southern California with quarterback guru Jordan Palmer "on

Josh Allen during 2019 training camp, a year older and a year wiser at QB. (Harry Scull Jr./Buffalo News)

mechanical stuff: sequencing in my shoulder to my hips, and little things like that." It included gathering most of the receivers who were on the roster in 2018 to catch passes from him in California before the start of free agency in March.

"I think taking initiative is something that a quote-unquote franchise quarterback is supposed to do," Allen said. "We worked for a few days, just to kind of home in on what we're doing in the playbook right before OTAs, obviously. Just trying to get back in the swing of things."

When the Bills' decision-makers did their assessments of Allen and the four other premiere college quarterbacks who would be selected in the first round in 2018 – Baker Mayfield, Sam Darnold, Lamar Jackson and Josh Rosen – they determined where each could make an immediate positive impact, where there was room for growth and shortcomings that might not necessarily be fixable.

Beane said the Bills were satisfied that all five first-rounders and "even some drafted after that" had the "physical ability to play in this league." Beyond that, they focused on intangibles, beginning with leadership. With this area, the Bills wouldn't leave anything to chance.

Beane, coach Sean McDermott and members of the Bills' player-personnel and coaching staffs took the first significant step in getting to know Allen better at the Senior Bowl college all-star game in Mobile, Ala. They spent about 30 minutes with him in a hotel boardroom. The session didn't go all that well.

"He was very nervous at the Senior Bowl, trying too hard to impress," Beane said.

The Bills chose not to meet with Allen at the NFL scouting combine, where teams get 15 minutes apiece to interview as many as 60 players, because they knew they required more time with Allen and wanted to use every available slot for non-quarterbacks.

A longer meeting with Allen was set for a couple of weeks later in Laramie, Wyoming. Besides Beane and McDermott, it included team owners Terry and Kim Pegula, assistant GM Joe Schoen, offensive coordinator Brian Daboll and then-quarterbacks coach David Culley.

The plan was for the whole group to have dinner with Allen at the Cavalryman Steakhouse. Reservations were set for 7:30 p.m. However, Allen's flight from Los Angeles was delayed due to bad weather.

Little did he realize that his handling of the circumstances would play a huge role in the Bills' evaluation of him. "That night was a testament to who Josh is," Beane said.

First, Allen impressed the Bills' hierarchy by staying in touch the whole time, providing updates on his ETA. Once it was known he wouldn't land in Denver until 8 p.m., and would still have a two-hour drive to Laramie, the Bills' contingent decided to go ahead and eat without him. But Allen assured the team he still planned to attend the meeting.

"He could have made a lot of excuses," Beane said. "I've had it happen before with players where something comes up. 'Hey, I can't make it. Can we just do this tomorrow?' Josh let us know his whereabouts every step of the way. 'I just landed in Denver. ... We're heading out. ... I'm an hour away.' That's a pro. We didn't have to reach out to him. So many young kids, including my own, will say, 'I'll be there when I get there.'"

The restaurant was scheduled to close at 10, before Allen's arrival, but the fact he was a local celebrity made it easy for Bills officials to convince the manager to keep it open.

Allen finally showed up a little after 10. Despite the late hour and long journey, he was upbeat and engaging. The hourlong conversation primarily focused on the quarterback's personal life, although there were football topics tied to a packet of material Daboll had sent with basics about the Bills' offense.

"That's crazy travel, but he was not acting tired," Beane said. "I'm sure, inside, he was going, 'Man, I'm trying to make a good impression on this team and the flights are screwed up.' But he came in and he was relaxed. He was calm. He knew the stuff. When Dabes was asking him questions, he spit it off."

Even more impressive, though, was how he behaved around everyone else in the restaurant.

Josh Allen's professionalism and focus on the task at hand were evident even during the pre-draft evaluation process. (Harry Scull Jr./Buffalo News)

"He spoke to every person in that place that he passed when he was walking in and walking out. 'Hey, how you doing?'" Beane said. "People know who Josh Allen is in Laramie, Wyo. You're watching how people are treated. He was very courteous. I didn't see a guy who was trying to impress. I saw a guy who was comfortable with where he was."

He still sees that guy.

"Josh has got a big personality," the GM said. "He fills the room."

"He's got all the things that you want for a franchise quarterback — leadership, charisma, players like him," CBS studio analyst and former New York Giants quarterback Phil Simms said. "He walks on the field, there's a tremendous presence with him, just like there is with Carson Wentz and Dak Prescott. They just have it."

Still, Allen recognizes he needs to make improvements in his game. Based on the many offseason additions the Bills made to upgrade the offensive line, at receiver and tight end, there's optimism that the supporting cast will do plenty to help bring the best out of him.

"You're going from the point of proving yourself to the point of establishing yourself," CBS studio analyst and former Pittsburgh Steelers coach Bill Cowher said. "He proved himself. Now, you have to establish yourself. Establishing yourself is your decision-making and saying, 'Now, what I want to do is continue to work on my accuracy and making all the right throws.'"

The Bills hired quarterbacks coach Ken Dorsey, a former NFL QB, with high expectations that he'll help elevate Allen's game.

"He's been fantastic," Allen said. "He comes into each meeting prepared with his list of notes. And he's not just like reiterating what (offensive coordinator Brian) Daboll says. And when Dabes is not there, Dorse has his own insights on certain concepts. Like, 'In this coverage, we really want to look at this. ... With my experience playing this, I always saw this guy.' Just little, subtle things like finding the right 'backer to ID and finding the right 'backer to look at. 'If his shoulder's turned one

way, flip your hips and throw it this way.' It's just little things like that have helped me out a lot."

One area where Allen knows he must make a significant jump is accuracy, a lingering flaw from college that only seemed to get worse based on his 52.8 completion percentage as a rookie. To that end, he took a critical look at every aspect of his game.

The first stat that jumped out at Allen was that he attempted more downfield throws than any other quarterback in the NFL. "And that kind of, in turn, hurts completion percentage and everybody knows that," he said. "Riskier, higher reward."

Allen still showed that tendency in the Bills' Aug. 23 preseason game against the Detroit Lions. He took a head-scratching risk when, while under pressure, he threw across his body to the middle of the field. The predictable interception was wiped out by a late hit on Allen.

What will it take for him to be more accurate with this throws this year?

"Being OK with three to four yards. That's what it comes down to," Allen said. "The competitor in me wants to throw the ball downfield and wants to get as many yards as possible and wants to force the ball into tight coverage on third down to pick up a first. But understanding how football is played now at the NFL level, and how situational football coincides with how the offense and the defense work together with special teams, I look at it in a different way now just being taught from Coach McDermott and Coach Daboll.

"I'm sure still, when I go on the field, there's going to be a few times where I try to force some stuff. Sometimes it's going to work out; sometimes it's not."

When it doesn't, Allen is confident he'll handle it the right way. After all, he has had 17 years to prepare for such moments. ∎

Josh Allen has a conversation with wide receiver John Brown during training camp in 2019. (Harry Scull Jr./Buffalo News)

'I'VE GOT A COUPLE GOOD MAGIC TRICKS'

Allen dishes on Wings, Will Ferrell, Superstitions, Golf and Cars

By Jay Skurski | September 3, 2019

As the starting quarterback of an NFL team, there's not much left unknown about Josh Allen.

The Buffalo Bills' second-year quarterback has become accustomed to the attention that comes with his high-profile position. Every national reporter who visits Orchard Park is looking to unearth a never-before-heard Allen story.

How he made it from the farmlands of tiny Firebaugh, Calif. – with a population of less than 8,000 – to his current job has been well documented. But what gives him the courage to pick Justin Bieber as his favorite musical artist? Here it is, along with more about Allen's life away from One Bills Drive …

The Buffalo News: Why is "Stepbrothers" the best Will Ferrell movie?

Josh Allen: "Him and John C. Reilly, they go very well together. Most of their early work is fantastic. I wouldn't say that their last piece of film was very good. I watched like 10 minutes of it, the Holmes and Watson one. Not good. I don't know, I just kind of grew up on that – me and my brother. We kind of related because of the challenges that they faced in that movie and ended up becoming best friends. Me and my brother are best friends, so I think that's probably why it's my favorite."

BN: That was a loaded question. It's my favorite, so I wanted to see if you agreed. If you want to pick another one, you can.

JA: "No. No. That one, and then I'm going to go with 'The Other Guys.' It's a very underrated movie. Not many people give it a chance. Him and Mark Wahlberg are fantastic in that one. He just plays an awkward, by the book guy, and he's got his alter ego of 'Gator.' I've watched Will Ferrell films over and over and over again, so I know them pretty well."

BN: So comedy movies, those are right up your alley?

JA: "Yeah. I'm not a big, serious, drama guy. I will do the action thrillers. Speaking of Mark Wahlberg, 'Shooter,' that's one of my favorite movies of all time, too. But comedy is probably my go-to."

BN: Your hidden talent is juggling? How'd that come about?

JA: "Just one day I did it. I had tennis balls and started trying it. It requires some good hand-eye coordination. I think it helps develop that, too. I did that when I was

Josh Allen takes a selfie after a day of training camp in 2019. (Harry Scull Jr./Buffalo News)

little. Going to swim meets, I just started juggling."

BN: Has this progressed to swords or flaming bowling pins or anything like that?

JA: "None of that. Not yet. Wait until football's done for that one."

BN: If you were on 'America's Got Talent,' would juggling impress Simon Cowell?

JA: "No, no. I can only do the regular three balls. That's not very impressive. I've got a couple good magic tricks – card tricks. I've won some money off those. So if you want to lose some money, let me know. That's probably it. There's not many other cool things I can do."

BN: That works. Magic plays well in Vegas.

JA: "Exactly."

BN: Tell me about your pregame routine, from the time you wake up to the ball kicks off. Is it the same every week?

JA: "Yeah. Wake up at 8:30. Obviously we stay at the team hotel, so it's get up, shower, brush your teeth, comb your hair. All that stuff. Put on your 'fit' (read: fancy clothes) for the walk through the tunnel. People take pictures there, so you've got to look kind of nice. I probably arrive here 2 1/2 hours before kickoff. I'll get into our game locker room and hang out in there. About two hours before kickoff, I'll go out on the field and throw for 30 minutes. Go back in and chill for 30, 35 minutes and then we're ready to go."

BN: You only listen to Elvis on your pregame playlist. What got you into that?

JA: "I don't really know. Last year, iTunes rereleased some of his essential music. I downloaded all of them, and I just go through that playlist when I'm out on the field. That's really all I play. Right when I'm in the locker room before we go out to the field, I'll turn on a couple other things to try to get me pumped up, but when I'm on the field in pregame, that's basically all I'm doing. Keeping a relaxed state of mind."

BN: Any superstitions?

JA: "Not really. Any time, I'm listening to music or radio, it's got to be an even number. If I'm watching TV, and someone turns the volume to 37, I can't focus until it's turned to 38 or 36. It has to. I'm not superstitious, but I guess I'm a little 'stitious.'"

BN: You pick Justin Bieber as your favorite musical artist. How much heat do you take in the locker room for that?

JA: "Not much. You can ask Lorenzo Alexander. He's got a little Google system, so every time in the St. John Fisher locker room, I'd walk in and be like, 'Hey Google, play Bieber.' Lorenzo didn't like it very much. I think the majority of our row enjoyed Bieber. I'd say half, if not more. Secretly, I think everybody likes him, they're just afraid to admit it."

BN: Is Bar Bill your spot for a restaurant in Buffalo if you had to pick one?

JA: "Obviously, wing mood, that would be my go-to. O.P. Social is pretty dang good. Their appetizers are fantastic. I go to Mangia quite a bit. I know the owner there. He's a really good guy. There's a few other spots. Ilio DiPaolo's is fantastic. I'm a big fan of Lucia's on the Lake in Hamburg. That one's good. And then downtown, Buffalo Chophouse and Toutant are my go-to. And SEAR."

BN: What's the ideal wing order?

JA: "I usually get 20. Half hot and half honey-butter BBQ, cajun style. I'm a spicy wing guy myself. Then you have to get fries with it. Have to. So it's not the healthiest diet, but when I have a cheat day, that's what I'm doing."

BN: Team owner Terry Pegula recommended Bar Bill to you, right?

JA: "Yeah. I was here on my (pre-draft) visit and got snowed in. So some of the guys here were like, 'Dude, you've got to go to Bar Bill.' So we went and hung out and they were the best wings I've ever had. When I got drafted here, I was like, 'I can't wait to get back to that spot.' "

BN: I never watched 'Game of Thrones,' but you picked it as your favorite TV show of all time.

JA: "Knowing now, I'd probably change that."

BN: It seemed like everyone had an opinion on the last season. What was yours?

JA: "It was terrible. I'm just kidding. The writers did such a good job of telling stories the previous seven seasons. Every season was 10 episodes or more. That

Josh Allen likes to have fun off the field too, watching Will Ferrell movies in his free time and listening to Elvis on his pre-game playlist. (Harry Scull Jr./Buffalo News)

was like what they were known for. Then all of a sudden this last season, it was six. It's like, 'OK, they're going to be like two hours each.' No, they were an hour each. Just the way it ended, I had so much more higher expectations for what should have happened or what could have happened. What they gave us, I was just like, I can't accept that. In my mind, I had thought of so many different possibilities. I had watched so many different videos of what could happen. So many different conspiracy theories about 'Game of Thrones.' I mean, I spent hours upon hours of diving into it. Then get into that final season, and it falls off a cliff. I know there are some people who liked the ending ... but I just wished they gave a little more back story of what happened. It seemed like they rushed the ending."

BN: Let's talk golf. What is it that attracted you to the sport, and how serious are you about it?

JA: "I love it. I tie it in with my affinity for throwing the football. I think it's very similar, what you feel when you throw a good pass and when you hit a good golf shot. Obviously when I'm throwing the ball, there are a few different variables. A guy is trying to tackle me, placement of the ball, things like that. Then when you're out on the golf course, it's wind, elevation. There are a lot of things that go into that, too, so I put it in that same context. I've been able to go to a couple Masters and a couple U.S. Opens now. I plan on going to as many as I can. I just love watching competitive golf and how they can shape the ball. There's so many things in a golf swing that can go wrong in the shortest amount of time. It's just crazy how some people have been so good in being able to do that consistently. I'm sure they kind of look at football players and quarterbacks in the same way, how they throw the ball and things like that, but personally, I find a similarity between those two things."

BN: You mentioned Tiger Woods was your favorite athlete growing up. What attracted you to him?

JA: "Not just his domination, but how he went about things. He was always like, 'I came here to win. I'm going to do whatever I can to win.' He wasn't afraid to voice his opinion on that matter. People were like, 'Why do you look so angry when you're golfing?' 'I'm not angry. I'm

focused. I came out here to win. If anybody came out here not to win, I think they're doing this for the wrong reasons.' Just the way that he forced himself to be the best golfer he can be."

BN: Outside of the food scene, what's your favorite thing you've done in this community?

JA: "Going to Niagara Falls was one of the most unbelievable experiences of my life. Went on the Maid of the Mist. I'm not a very nostalgic person, but being down there and seeing how big the falls actually are. It was kind of surreal to be in that position. That was cool. ... The people are just fantastic. Anywhere I go, it's friendly faces, friendly people. I don't really go out much. I just kind of hang out at the house."

BN: You got a chance to go to Monaco this offseason. How was that?

JA: "We were there for 2 1/2 days and most of it was flying. I got the opportunity to go and I took it. I was asked four days prior to it, and I didn't have any plans. That was one of the bucket list things I had on my list. I got to get in a Ferrari and drive the track with a professional driver. I got in there and was like, 'Go as fast as you can. I want it all.' I took a video of the whole thing. Just the experience of being there – this was my first time in Europe, too, so seeing how different it was over there, but how much people respect that sport (Allen was there for the Formula One Monaco Grand Prix). I got to understand a little better about the technology and what goes into these cars. It's just insane how much thought, technology and money is put into these cars. How loud they are, how fast they are, how respected the drivers are from everybody that goes to these events. It was an eye-opener just to show me there are other things out there."

BN: Are you a big car guy?

JA: "I have a liking for cars, but I don't plan on buying many. I do enjoy the sound and the look, though."

BN: What was your first big purchase after you got drafted?

JA: "Probably my car. It's a Range Rover. I grew up always wanting one. I was at a (San Francisco) Giants game and I saw Barry Bonds in a Range Rover when I was like 8 years old. Ever since then, I was like, 'That's

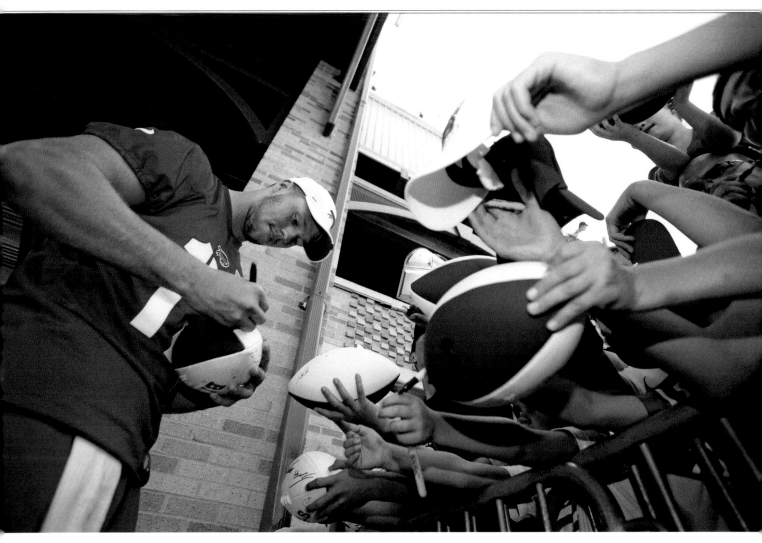

While an intense competitor between the lines, Josh Allen's relaxed and relatable personality is a big hit with fans. (Harry Scull Jr./Buffalo News)

the coolest thing ever.' So I did that. I got the Sport, so it goes pretty fast. I probably drive it a little faster than I actually should, but it feels pretty good."

BN: How rewarding was that, to make one of your dreams come true?

JA: "As athletes, we work pretty hard to get where we're at. To step back and do something for yourself once, that's kind of what I did. I got the car of my dreams. That's really all I need. I've got a house here in Buffalo, and I really don't need much else. I'm trying to be smart with my money – save most of it, invest in the right way and when the time comes, take care of my family when needed."

BN: Finally, what's your favorite spot to go to get away from football?

JA: "I'm a big Southern California guy. I live in central California, and I go back there, and it gets pretty hectic with my family and people wanting to see you and take you to dinner. It's tough because I always put on extra weight when I go there, because I'm always going to dinner. When I'm in Southern California, it's just on the beach. No one really cares about anything else. They're not really big on football. They're just into their beaches and their weather, so that's probably my go-to spot." ■

THAT'S THE TICKET

Bills Leave Nothing to Chance in Clinching Playoff Spot

By Vic Carucci | December 16, 2019

The Buffalo Bills did it right.

No waiting another game or even two to punch their ticket to the postseason. No leaving anything to chance.

The Bills had their shot to win and become no worse than a fifth seed in the AFC playoffs, and they cashed in with a 17-10 victory against the Pittsburgh Steelers at Heinz Field. It marks the Bills' second postseason appearance in the last three years.

"To be in the playoffs in two of the three years now that we've been here, (although) we still have a lot of work to do, I'm extremely grateful and humble just to be a part of it," coach Sean McDermott said.

The Bills, who improved their record to 10-4 for their first 10-win season since 1999, finally broke out of an offensive malaise midway through the fourth quarter when they drove 70 yards in six plays for the winning points on a 14-yard Josh Allen touchdown pass to a wide-open Tyler Kroft.

Though the Bills had a chance to put the game away when Jordan Poyer intercepted Devlin Hodges in the end zone with 1:54 left, the Steelers had one more chance after forcing the Bills to punt. They put a scare into the Bills, driving to their 26 before Hodges threw another interception in the end zone, this time to Levi Wallace.

It was Kroft's first TD since joining the Bills in the offseason as a free agent, and since he had two with the Cincinnati Bengals in their victory against the Baltimore Ravens in the final game of the 2017 season that allowed Buffalo to end a 17-year playoff drought.

"I had a corner route," Kroft said. "I saw the coverage and I knew, when Motor (Devin Singletary) went to the flat, I was going to be open on the out break. So I was just trying to make sure I was just putting myself in position to be there for Josh."

Sure, even in a loss, the Bills would have had been able to land a playoff bid with a victory in either of their final two games: next Saturday against the New England Patriots at Foxborough, Mass., or their Dec. 29 regular-season finale against the New York Jets at New Era Field.

Taking care of business in Pittsburgh, though, removed the burden of trying to win at Gillette Stadium, where the Bills only have two victories since 2014 — both while Tom Brady either sat out a half or the entire game. The Bills still have a shot at the AFC East title if they beat the Patriots and the Jets, and the Pats lose their season finale against Miami.

Sunday night's triumph also took away a scenario where, if a Jets win were needed for a postseason berth, the Bills would have entered the game on a three-game losing streak.

"Obviously, you kind of get that monkey off your back so you don't start playing tight," linebacker Lorenzo Alexander said. "You lose this one and you've got to play New England and then it's almost a must-win if you're going into that last week trying to get a playoff berth.

"And who knows what happens? The Jets might want to play us real hard and then we don't make it in."

Josh Allen and the Bills clinched the team's first 10-win season since 1999 with a 17-10 win over the Steelers. (James P. McCoy/Buffalo News)

Those worries are gone, thanks in no small measure to the Bills taking the approach that if the Steelers were going to beat them, they would have to do so on the shaky arm of Hodges, their undrafted rookie quarterback.

The Steelers (8-6) had been doing their best this season to minimize Hodges' passing since he replaced Mason Rudolph four games ago. They were leaning heavily on the run, while Hodges had not thrown more than 21 passes in three victories.

On Sunday night, he attempted a season-high 38 throws – and wound up with four interceptions and was sacked four times.

The first sign that this game would go as scripted for a Bills victory came on the Steelers' first drive when Hodges, mustering all the effort he could, heaved a pass that Tre'Davious White intercepted at the Buffalo 25. The Bills couldn't cash in on the turnover, but the tone was set.

The Steelers continued to have issues moving the ball with Hodges. That led to Jordan Berry's punting the ball straight up for only 22 yards, setting up the Bills at the Steelers' 40. This time, the Bills made the most of the opportunity, driving to a 1-yard Josh Allen touchdown run to take a 7-0 lead early in the second quarter.

The Steelers' kicking game isn't all bad. Placekicker Chris Boswell has been having a strong season, and he came through in a big way after the Bills' scoring drive by connecting on a 49-yard field goal to cut the margin to 7-3 with 11:26 left in the second quarter. Hodges help set up the score with a 34-yard pass to James Washington.

The Bills had seemingly hurt themselves with sloppiness of their own late in the half. Allen threw a pass that was high and Cole Beasley allowed it to bounce off his hands, resulting in an interception by cornerback Steven Nelson at the Bills' 20. A facemask penalty by Kevin Johnson moved the ball to the 10.

However, on the next play, Trent Murphy forced a fumble that Poyer recovered at the Buffalo 9 with 1:53 remaining in the second quarter. The Bills were content to get conservative and stay on the ground while allowing the first-half clock to run out.

The Steelers began to show some offensive life at the start of the second half. Hodges connected on a 29-yard pass to Diontae Johnson, who fumbled but teammate Tevin Jones recovered at the Bills' 38. James Conner ran 17 yards to the Bills' 10. Two plays later, Hodges rolled to his right and threw to a wide-open Conner for an 11-yard touchdown to put the Steelers in front, 10-7, with 11:18 left in the third quarter.

The Bills' sloppy ways continued in the third quarter. Singletary had a promising run deep in Steeler territory turn disastrous when T.J. Watt punched the ball out from behind. Cornerback Mike Hilton recovered at the Steelers' 31.

But the Steelers went nowhere and another poor punt by Berry put the Bills at their own 36 with 6:48 left in the third quarter. The Bills did nothing with the opportunity, as the Steelers' defensive front kept its mostly firm control of the line of scrimmage.

No problem. The Bills' defense came to the rescue. Again.

White intercepted his second Hodges pass of the night and returned it 49 yards to the Steelers' 18. The Bills squandered an chance, thanks to both their inability to win battles up front and general offensive ineptitude. In one case, a broken play that was supposed to have been a pass became a three-yard loss on a run by Frank Gore — one of six consecutive runs after the turnover.

The Bills wound up settling for a 36-yard Stephen Hauschka field goal to tie the game at 10-10 with 12:23 left in the fourth quarter and Buffalo was on its way to its fourth comeback in the fourth quarter this season.

"I mean, shoot, all you can ask for in this league is an opportunity, it's hard to get there," fullback Patrick DiMarco said. "We've got our spot now. It's just time to keep moving forward, get the division, get a home game in Buffalo and just keep getting better every week. Offensively, we didn't play completely like we wanted to today. We did enough, so we have to keep on keeping on." ∎

The 2019 playoff berth was the second in three years for the Bills and a stepping stone to bigger things for the franchise. (James P. McCoy/Buffalo News)

HALF FULL OR HALF EMPTY?

In 2019, Allen Improved in Almost Every Category

By Mark Gaughan | January 9, 2020

Buffalo Bills fans can spend all offseason debating their perspective on quarterback Josh Allen.

Is the glass half full or half empty?

Bills offensive coordinator Brian Daboll has no hesitation about where he comes down. In fact, Daboll's glass is way more than half full on Allen.

"Just overall improvement is what I like," Daboll told The Buffalo News after the final game of the regular season. "He's very level headed. I appreciate really everything about him, how he comes to work. I appreciate his professionalism, his accountability, how he deals with the entire organization from the top down. And how he is off the field. I have a lot of respect for him as a young player and how he approaches the job."

The bottom line on Allen's season: He got better in almost every measurable way over his rookie season.

His completion percentage rose from 52.8% as a rookie to 58.8%. That 6% rise was the third best improvement of any quarterback in the NFL, behind only Baltimore's Lamar Jackson (up 7.9% to 66.1%) and Tennessee's Ryan Tannehill (up 6.1% to 70.3%).

Glass half empty? Allen still ranks 32nd in the NFL in completion percentage.

Still, Allen's across-the-board improvements are undeniable.

He was up from 32nd to 23rd in passing yards, from 31st to 18th in TD percentage, from 32nd to 16th in interception rate and from 32nd to 24th in passer rating.

More importantly, his record as a starter went from 5-6 to 10-6. He tied for first in the NFL in game-winning drives (five) and in fourth-quarter comebacks (four).

And Allen cut way back on his interceptions after a three-interception game against the New England Patriots in September. Over the last 12 games of the regular season, Allen produced 23 touchdowns (counting rushing TDs) and three interceptions.

Allen produced 18 TDs and 12 INTs as a rookie. This year, he had 29 TDs and 9 INTs. That TD-to-INT differential of plus-20 was ninth best in the NFL. How much more could he be expected to improve in one season?

Allen's deep passing did not improve. He completed just 25.7% on passes 20-plus yards beyond the line of scrimmage, and his rate ranked fourth worst in the league (adjusting for drops).

"We have a lot of faith in him in anything that we call, short, intermediate or deep," Daboll said. "At the end of the day, that's why Brandon Beane drafted him, and we're happy that he did."

On throws of under 20 yards – which is the vast majority of passes in the NFL – Allen's accuracy improved from 65.9% as a rookie to 71.9% this year.

Given how much attention was paid to Allen's accuracy coming out of college, it's not going to be easy for him to shake the inaccuracy label. Every time he misses an easy one – remember the too-low swing pass to a wide-open Patrick DiMarco in Pittsburgh – it reinforces the reputation.

Allen makes the leap for the first down over Houston Texans linebacker Zack Cunningham in Buffalo's 22-19 loss in the AFC wild-card playoff game. (James P. McCoy/Buffalo News)

"Look, trust me, every quarterback's going to have some of those," Daboll said of the incompletion to DiMarco.

Obviously, a lot more goes into accuracy numbers than throwing the ball.

Like most second-year quarterbacks, Allen still is in a developmental stage in terms of reading defenses. He missed open plays in the Houston wild-card game. At times against man coverage, which the Bills saw more of as the season wore on, Allen takes too long to get off his first read.

Daboll said Allen will have a natural progression on getting to his secondary routes better.

"It's time on task," Daboll said. "We have a variety of option routes in the game plan. It's about body language and time on task with throws and anticipation and reps.

"When you have an option route with the quarterback, you have to be so in tune with the body language of the receiver because there's different types of routes," Daboll said.

Another year working with the same receivers is only going to improve the efficiency of Allen and the offense, Daboll said.

"When you have option routes, it's the receiver's decision. So the throw and timing is not going to be just like that," he said, snapping his fingers. "Versus you want to run a curl route. You know where he's going to be at 12 yards or 14 yards or 16 yards. He's going to be on the inside edge of the numbers, he's going to be 3 yards from the sideline, or he's going to be 2 yards inside the numbers and you can let it rip.

"When you have players who have short-space quickness, like Cole (Beasley), Motor (Devin Singletary), guys like that, you're relying on their eyes and how they see it. That's how it works."

Allen's most impressive throws get fans, teammates and coaches excited. Those plays scream "elite ability."

One example was a 29-yard pass to Beasley early in the win at Dallas. The Bills were backed up on their own 2-yard line, facing third and 10. Allen slid to his right, stepped up and made a laser strike into a tight window.

"Very, very impressive," Daboll said. "The ability to move in the pocket and keep his eyes downfield. It was a tight window throw. He did a good job with that read."

Then there was the big arm strength he showed beating Miami's Cover 2 defense with a 40-yard laser to John Brown for a TD.

"He's an instinctive player but he's also a smart player," Daboll said. "He has a good feel for defenses. He has a good feel for in-game adjustments and the things that happen within the game that he sees. It's all stuff we continue to work on. I've said it numerous times, I'm very happy with his progress."

Arguably the best throw of Allen's season was the 53-yard bomb to Brown in New England, when the QB anticipated the route and let the pass go before Brown made his break and just before getting hit in the pocket.

"That was an example too of trust in his player," Daboll said. "Impressive. But that's also an example of what's helped Josh: John Brown. What's helped Josh is Cole Beasley, Frank Gore. Devin Singletary, Mitch Morse, Jon Feliciano, Quinton Spain."

"I want him to turn it loose," Daboll said. "I want him to trust what he sees. You can get second-guessed all you want playing the quarterback position. But he's the one who has to make split-second decisions. I trust him to make those."

The challenge for Allen: Improving to the same degree again in Year Three. ■

Josh Allen improved in most major passing categories in 2019, a key progression on his way to stardom in the 2020 season. (Mark Mulville/Buffalo News)

A FRANCHISE
QUARTERBACK

STAMP OF APPROVAL

Allen Verifies He's a Franchise QB as Bills Go to 2-0

By Vic Carucci | September 20, 2020

Even if it's only two games into the season and 30 into his NFL career, Josh Allen has put the official "verified" stamp on his status as a franchise quarterback.

There's ample support for this, beginning with the staggering 417 yards and four touchdowns, with no interceptions, that he threw in the Buffalo Bills' 31-28 victory against the Miami Dolphins. It came seven days after his first career 300-yard passing game, against the New York Jets.

But the stat that's even better is this: Only four quarterbacks have thrown for 700-plus yards, six-plus touchdowns and zero interceptions in the first two weeks of the season, and Allen is one of them. The others? Peyton Manning, Tom Brady, and Patrick Mahomes. That's elite company.

Get that checkbook warmed up, Brandon Beane. You know you're going to be doing your biggest contract extension of them all in the not-too-distant future. Because Allen is, without question, the answer for whom the Bills have been waiting seemingly forever.

"He's got ice water in his veins," Sean McDermott, who is normally not big on hyperbole, told reporters on a postgame video call from Miami Gardens, Fla. "There's no moment too big for him."

The final 15 minutes of a game certainly aren't. Allen, who shared the NFL lead for fourth-quarter comebacks

in 2019, picked up where he left off by leading the Bills from a 20-17 deficit early in fourth Sunday with touchdown passes to rookie receiver Gabe Davis and veteran wideout John Brown, finishing drives of 75 and 71 yards. Allen now has seven fourth-quarter comebacks and has led nine game-winning drives.

Being without two of his team's best defensive players, injured linebackers Tremaine Edmunds and Matt Milano, and the negative impact it had on that side of the ball couldn't rattle Allen, either. Nor did a 32-minute delay early in the second half because of lightning.

Consistently rising to the occasion is what franchise QBs do.

"That was true from the very start when we got him here quite honestly," McDermott said. "And I'm proud of the way the guys are developing a mindset. Adversity we faced last week, all the way back to starting training camp with Covid and adversity we saw last week, the adversity we saw today, a lot of challenges. And Josh is the leader and he does a great job leading by example."

Allen's production Sunday was only the second time in Bills history a quarterback has thrown for four-plus touchdowns and 415-plus yards. The first was when Joe Ferguson threw for 419 yards and five TDs against the Dolphins in 1983. Allen's 417 yards were the most by a Bill since Drew Bledsoe had the same total against the Raiders in 2002.

Allen became one of only four quarterbacks who have thrown for 700-plus yards, six-plus touchdowns and zero interceptions in the first two weeks of a season with his start to 2020. (Associated Press)

Oh, Allen had his occasional rough spots. An overthrow here. An out-of-reach pass there. An ill-advised sack.

Those plays are going to happen, just as with his two fumbles and the overthrow on a sure touchdown against the Jets. There's no need to obsess over them. The three other guys on that list of superlative efforts in the first two games of the season have had their share of blunders, too. You forgive them, because you see more of the plays that make them great.

 Allen is doing exactly that. In two games, he has taken command of the offense, and the team, in ways that weren't seen in either of his previous two years. He is a little older, a little wiser. And can we finally put to rest all of the handwringing about his lack of long-ball accuracy?

"I'm asking you," Allen said to me after the game.

Three passes of 46 or more yards Sunday should have taken care of that. Allen threw for 246 yards on pass plays of 20-plus yards, completing 7 of 8. Last season, he was among the worst in the league in those situations with a 24.1% completion rate, according to Pro Football Focus.

"Josh is doing what Josh do, man," running back Devin Singletary said when told of Allen's stat line. "It's amazing. I just want to see him keep on getting better. That's really what is. He's a general ... we are behind him 100%."

Stefon Diggs' eight catches for 153 yards and a TD are the epitome of what Allen's bombs-away skills are about. The constant threat Diggs poses for game-breaking plays terrifies opposing defenses – "It's scary. I would hate to be on the other side," Singletary said – and creates openings for the rest of the pass-catchers. It also allows Brian Daboll to be highly aggressive with his play-calling, as he has the past two weeks, going full throttle to the very end.

It takes a top-notch quarterback to make everything go, and Allen fits the bill. Finally.

"I think it's an attitude that we just have," Allen said. "We believe in our playmakers here and coach

Daboll's not the one to shy away from putting the ball in my hands."

Even more important is that McDermott won't hold Daboll back.

The head coach's philosophy is deeply rooted in defense, which tends to lead to more conservative thinking on the offensive side. The typical instruction a defensive-minded head coach gives his offensive coordinator is, "Whatever you do, don't add to the burden of the defense."

Without Edmunds and Milano, McDermott had ample reason to fret over putting additional pressure on the Bills' defenders. McDermott never flinched.

"I think some defensive head coaches take the approach of continuing to pad their side of the ball and they like winning, 11-9 ... and having no hair, I guess," McDermott said. He lifted his cap to show his bald head and gave the smile of a coach with a 2-0 record.

"Whereas, for me, I don't like winning, 11-9. I like winning. But I just feel like, to have a good football team that can sustain success, you need to have a balanced football team. And, so, Brandon Beane and his staff did a great job of continuing to look offensively what we could add to what we had. I think you're seeing the result of some of that."

That's because the Bills have the most important piece of all at quarterback. ∎

Wide receiver John Brown and Josh Allen were in a celebratory mood in Buffalo's win over Miami, which gave them a 2-0 record on the season. (AP Images)

JOSH'S JAQS

Cereal Sales Robust After Strong Start to the Season

By Vic Carucci | September 24, 2020

Josh Allen's cereal is, as with pretty much everything else connected with the Buffalo Bills quarterback, a red-hot item.

"Josh's Jaqs" are flying off grocery store shelves, according to Ty Ballou, president and chief executive officer of Public Label Brands, the Pittsburgh-based company that specializes in food items branded by pro athletes.

Allen has designated 17% of the proceeds to Buffalo's Oishei Children's Hospital.

Ballou, whose company produced "Flutie Flakes" when Doug Flutie was with the Bills, told The Buffalo News on Wednesday that, within the last week or so, 75,000 boxes of the cereal were shipped to about 60 Wegmans stores, including locations in North Carolina. Ballou said sales are "on the same trajectory" as those for "Mahomes Magic Crunch," named after Kansas City Chiefs quarterback Patrick Mahomes.

Ballou said 300,000 boxes of Mahomes' cereal were shipped to 35 stores in 12 weeks.

"I can't say (Allen's cereal) is going to get there," Ballou said by phone. "But it is starting out exactly the way Mahomes' did."

Allen said he didn't initiate the idea of having a cereal named after him.

"It's something that was just kind of brought to my attention," he said in a video call with reporters Wednesday. "It wasn't something that I was looking to do, but it's just a cool opportunity. The name was kind of an ode to 'Flutie Flakes,' Josh's Jaqs. I love the alliteration ... it's just really cool.

"As a kid, that's something that you kind of dream of is being an athlete and being on a cereal box. It's something that people get and they start their day and they look at me on a cereal box. It's definitely weird, but it's a cool thing and something to cross off the bucket list." ∎

Josh Allen's cereal, "Josh's Jaqs," saw an early spike in sales that coincided with Allen's quick start to the 2020 season. (Harry Scull Jr. / Buffalo News)

'A COMPLETELY DIFFERENT QUARTERBACK'

NFL Analysts, Draft Experts Revisit Allen Projections

By Jason Wolf | October 2, 2020

In April 2018, in his final mock draft, NFL Network analyst Mike Mayock predicted the Bills would trade up into the top 10.

"And with that pick," Mayock said on television, "the Buffalo Bills take the quarterback with the most upside in this draft, Josh Allen. Dude is 6-5, 237. He's the same size as Carson Wentz, with bigger arm talent, and he's a better athlete. Now, he's not ready to play as early as Carson Wentz, but I'm telling you, out of maybe any player in this draft, his upside might be the highest."

Today, Mayock is the general manager of the Las Vegas Raiders, who will host Allen and the undefeated Bills on Sunday at Allegiant Stadium.

Allen, the AFC Offensive Player of the Month for September.

Allen, who's tops in the conference and second in the league in passing yards.

Allen, the only player in Bills history to account for four-plus touchdowns in consecutive games.

Allen, the only player in NFL history with at least 1,000 passing yards, 10 passing touchdowns and two rushing touchdowns in the first three weeks of a season.

"Now here's play action," Mayock said 2½ years ago, evaluating film of Allen at Wyoming. "Watch him climb the pocket, and this is what I'm talking about, 'arm talent.' Nobody makes that throw that way in the entire NFL. … This is 40 yards, on the run, to his left, to a tiny window. Are you kidding me?

"Wyoming used him in the run game an awful lot, and he's a load. This is a real good football player. The issue is he throws late, off his back foot, and the question of anticipation, timing and accuracy is what's going to take him a little while to get used to."

Not everyone agreed with Mayock's analysis.

For every like-minded evaluator – such as ESPN draft guru Mel Kiper Jr., who mocked Allen at No. 1 overall and said "stats are for losers" while shrugging at the quarterback's lousy 56.2 completion percentage in college – there were critics.

Some prognosticators saw Allen as a junior college kid who couldn't hit the broad side of a barn in his two seasons as a starter at Wyoming, which went 15-9 against FBS competition with Allen behind center and didn't exactly dominate the Mountain West Conference.

The Football Outsiders Almanac called Allen a "parody of an NFL quarterback prospect."

Pro Football Focus ranked him the 35th-best prospect overall and No. 6 quarterback in his class, behind Baker Mayfield, Sam Darnold, Josh Rosen,

The pre-draft evaluations of Allen ran the gamut, but those who believed in his talent and upside were ultimately vindicated. (Harry Scull Jr./Buffalo News)

Lamar Jackson and Mason Rudolph, who went in the third round to the Steelers.

WalterFootball.com cited scouts who compared Allen to Ravens bust Kyle Boller.

That was then.

This week, an apology form for Allen's haters began circulating on social media.

The Buffalo News took it a few steps farther, reaching out to national NFL analysts and draft experts to compare their thoughts on Allen the prospect – before the Bills traded up to select him with the seventh overall pick in 2018 – and Allen the early season NFL MVP candidate, which he looks like today.

For some, it was an opportunity to take a victory lap. For others, a chance to explain themselves and atone for their sins.

(In reality, even the harshest predictions seem relatively fair and well-reasoned.)

MEL KIPER JR., ESPN

THEN: "You have to look beyond the stats. Stats are for losers in my opinion in a lot of ways. The kid won. You say what was his record? When he was out there, they won football games. … No other quarterback in the NFL that started this year outside of Josh McCown came out of college with a lower career completion percentage. I get that. I get that stat. If you don't like that stat, nobody would even take him in the first round if that's a bothersome thing. I think you have to look at the tape, watch every throw and see how many of those were on Josh Allen just not being accurate, not precise. How many were on the receivers, on the line or whatever. I think they'll find that completion percentage was a little misleading."

NOW: "I saw a lot of Brett Favre in Josh, where he'd try to throw that 100 mph fastball sometimes when he didn't need to, and became a little impatient and had sometimes too much faith in that cannon arm. The one thing he needed to work on is being less reckless. And

that is about knowing situations in a game, which I think he's done a much better job. … He's not finished yet. What you're seeing with him, this isn't the best Josh Allen that he's going to be.

"All the haters want to be correct, so that's never going to end. He's always going to have that, because people never want to admit they're wrong. And I get that. But I was trying to defend him objectively, point out what he needs to improve, but defend him against these haters who were just relentless. They were relentless over his first two years, even into this year. I heard people mentioning quarterbacks in July and August and they never mentioned Josh Allen. They did everything in their power to keep him out of their conversation of one of the bright young quarterbacks in the league. They didn't even mention Josh Allen, a lot of people, and I'd get sick and almost turn it off. It made me disgusted, because it was like they'd go out of their way to never mention Josh Allen's name, and if they do it's in a negative way.

"I think most of it is people didn't like him coming out, and that's the main thing. A lot of these people, I call them 'ana-lie-tics.' Analytics can lie. There are always outliers. So all the analytics people hated Josh Allen. I guess they'll keep hating until they can't hate anymore."

DANIEL JEREMIAH, NFL Network

THEN: "Allen has the most upside of any QB in this draft, but he also has a lower floor than some of his fellow signal-callers."

NOW: "Coming out of the draft, you knew about the size and the athletic ability and arm strength. All the traits, right? He was totally a 'traits' guy. And that was what jumped out to you. Now, everybody knows the whole story about how (bad) the Wyoming team was, so he had to do a lot more for that team than he necessarily has to do for the Bills, in terms of the pressure that he was under, the lack of weapons that he had, all those things.

Josh Allen's winning personality and connection to his teammates have played big roles in his on-field success. (Harry Scull Jr./Buffalo News)

"He was fighting an uphill battle and that caused him to force throws, that caused him to be a little reckless at times, both trying to squeeze balls in miniscule windows when he wasn't under pressure, and when he was under pressure, he'd have to escape and make Superman-type plays. That was a totally different scenario than where he is right now in Buffalo and with the team that they've put around him, you're starting to see him really blossom.

"I think he's got a ton of trust in the guys he has around him, so you're seeing him throw with anticipation and timing, something that he never really did a lot of earlier. That's what to me jumps out the most. I'm not surprised that he's making unbelievable throws. What surprises me is how consistent he's been, and for the most part has avoided those kinds of reckless tendencies that he might have had in the past."

SAM MONSON, Pro Football Focus

THEN: "Allen can make big-time throws and has unquestionably the best arm strength of the draft class, but he also misses far too many routine throws that hurt his efficiency. ... Even adjusting for screens, Allen's a dramatically more inaccurate passer than the other top prospects in this draft. Inaccuracy isn't always a constant, and players have improved it in the NFL or simply offset it with big plays, either of which is possible for him, but if he can't do that, he may have a far higher bust potential than the other top prospects who have a higher baseline of passing."

NOW: "Josh Allen so far this year has been a different guy from anything we've seen before. I think he's taken consistent small steps forward in the NFL, but this year it's been a leap, and even in the areas he was deficient in before.

"His two biggest weaknesses in the past have been general accuracy – not that he isn't capable of accurate passes, but that over a large sample size he will miss more passes than most quarterbacks – and tendency

to make mistakes. Those were the reasons PFF didn't love him as a prospect or a QB over his first two years in the league, because those two things tend not to be massively improved upon at the NFL level.

"This year in particular, neither have been problems. His completion rate speaks for itself, but even his adjusted completion rate (adjusted for drops, spikes, nontargeted passes) is 79.1%, good enough for 13th in the league. It hasn't become a strength, necessarily, but it is no longer a weakness. Similarly, the mistakes are still there, but they are a much smaller percentage of his play, and of course, his ability to make big plays and wow people is still there.

"We're still only three games into the season, and there are some numbers that suggest he might regress a little over the year, but at this point his negatives are very small if this is the player that we have moving forward. He still has a tendency to get into trouble trying to make something happen, and sometimes it costs him, but he more than offsets that right now with the plays he DOES make."

PETE PRISCO, CBS Sports

THEN: "I am starting to believe the talk in scouting circles that Allen will be the (No. 1 overall) pick. He should be."

NOW: "I was bullish on Josh Allen from the get-go. He was my No. 1 quarterback in that draft class. I thought all the accuracy issues he had at Wyoming, I used to joke around, he threw to bouncers and bartenders. It was hard to evaluate him.

"I knew he would improve on his mechanics, and he has. He's got the 'it' factor. He's big, he's strong, he's tough, he's physical. He's gotten better at going through his progressions. I thought the first couple of years, he'd go 'one, two,' and get out. I think he's doing a better job of going 'one, two, three, four,' and then maybe getting out. He's got the big arm. He can make all the throws. Accuracy was an issue the first couple of years. And I

The athleticism Josh Allen displayed in college was unquestioned, but several scouts and analysts expressed concern about his accuracy as a passer. (Harry Scull Jr./Buffalo News)

think he's improved on that a great deal.

"Now, Lamar Jackson is in that draft class, too. But I thought when Allen came in, he'd be the best quarterback in that draft class. And right now, to be honest with you, he's playing better than Lamar Jackson."

CHARLIE CAMPBELL, WalterFootball.com

THEN: "When Allen is playing well, he looks like a young (Ben) Roethlisberger with his powerful arm, mobility and ability to make big plays with his feet. When Allen is struggling – throwing inaccurately and making poor decisions – his style of play is reminiscent of Boller."

NOW: "There is no doubt that Allen is vastly improved from the player he was at Wyoming. When you think back to how he played against Oregon and Iowa, there has been a striking transformation.

"The No. 1 issue for Allen to improve entering the NFL was accuracy, and he has made remarkable strides there. His footwork has greatly improved, and that has led to him having more consistent precision and ball placement. Along with his mechanics, Allen's poise and ability to excel in the clutch have grown exponentially.

"Allen's improvement is a credit to him, the Bills coaches, and the front office for putting in place talent allowing him to thrive."

ROB RANG, NFLDraftScout.com

THEN: Rang rated Allen the No. 3 quarterback prospect in his draft class and slotted him to Buffalo, writing "Allen's 56.2 career completion percentage is worrisome but is not much lower than the numbers put up by former top three picks Matt Ryan (59.9) and Matthew Stafford (57.1) in college."

NOW: "My evaluation of Josh Allen hasn't changed that much. He remains the ultratalented, ultracompetitive dual-threat quarterback I scouted in person at the Senior Bowl and saw play through peaks and valleys at Wyoming.

"He remains less accurate than many of the starting quarterbacks in today's NFL but that does not give him enough credit for his remarkable combination of size, speed and strength – both as a passer and in fighting through would-be tacklers in the pocket and on the run. His ability to attack every level of the defense makes him one of the most difficult passers in the NFL for opposing clubs to face.

"The Bills have done a nice job of surrounding him with the game-breaking speed to take full advantage of his skill set."

JORDAN REID, The Draft Network

THEN: "The physical traits are obviously there with Josh Allen. Footwork, mental processing speed, pocket awareness, and accuracy need to improve. Lots of high and low flashes, but many teams will value him as a huge project that could be molded into a productive NFL starter."

NOW: "I wasn't a big fan of Josh coming out, just because the accuracy is something that's so hard to improve with quarterbacks. You very rarely see a guy improve on his accuracy. I had a second-round grade on him. ... But, man, he's doing a phenomenal job now. And I think accuracy is one of the big points that he's improved on the most.

"He just didn't have adequate weapons at Wyoming … and I think that's a big difference, getting receivers that create a lot of separation, because he's a guy that's always struggled with ball placement. The Bills got receivers that create these bigger windows, so he has a lot more margin for error.

"He's also become less of a risk taker throughout his career, even though he's always going to have that daredevil in him, like we saw in the playoffs last year."

AARON SCHATZ, Football Outsiders/ESPN

THEN: "I would rather have Tyrod Taylor quarterbacking my team over the next four years than Josh Allen."

NOW: "We have him No. 2 so far in passing value behind Russell Wilson. ... I don't know if he can continue at this level. I doubt it."

Through hard work, a dedication to his craft and a supportive coaching staff and organization, Josh Allen thrived in a Bills uniform. According to ESPN analyst Mel Kiper Jr.: "What you're seeing with him, this isn't the best Josh Allen that he's going to be." (James P. McCoy/Buffalo News)

"Ryan Fitzpatrick had a very similar start in 2011. He was older at that point, obviously. But he had a very similar start, exactly the same by our DYAR metric (Defense-adjusted Yards Above Replacement), in his first three games in 2011. And then it fell apart. So nothing is set in stone here. But Allen's been a completely different quarterback than he ever was before, or that you ever could have expected him to be. So far. In the first three games.

"If he's truly going to play at this level for the rest of the year, it would be an almost unprecedented turnaround. More power to him if he does it. Everything with statistical analysis is about probability, right? So there was always the probability that he would get his act together. It just was really low. … And so for him to pass like this is just phenomenal.

"I don't think he's going to be the second-best passer for the rest of the year, but I wouldn't be surprised if he was the 12th-best passer for the rest of the year. And that's a big step forward from where we thought he was. You've got yourself a real, live, NFL, above average starting quarterback." ∎

A SPECIAL BOND

Allen Says Donations in Honor of 'Grammy' are 'Unbelievable'

By Vic Carucci | November 11, 2020

At some point, we stop being what the outside world only chooses to see.

A quarterback is so much more than a quarterback. He's a person with a family, with people he loves and who love him. It's a bond that doesn't change with time or the fact countless others know his name and recognize his face and pay attention to all that he does and says.

That was the Josh Allen who spoke with reporters on a video call Wednesday.

Most of the discussion had nothing to do with the Buffalo Bills' 7-2 start or what sort of encore Allen might have for his lights-out performance against the Seattle Seahawks. His being named the AFC Offensive Player of the Week came up, but only in the context of whether it carried more meaning because he had played the game 24 hours after the passing of his grandmother, Patricia Allen.

On Wednesday, the main topic wasn't football.

It was the woman who a 6-foot-5-inch, 237-pound, tough-as-nails, 24-year-old professional athlete still calls his "Grammy."

"Just the sweetest, nicest lady you'd ever meet," Allen said in his first comments to the media since his grandmother's death became public Sunday. "Not a single mean bone in her body."

"Grammy" died unexpectedly Saturday, not long after her 80th birthday. The pain was still evident four days later.

Allen seemed to relish the opportunity to share what she meant to him and his family, to let the many people who have passed along their condolences directly and indirectly understand how big of a loss this was to him and his family.

This was the woman who cooked "the most amazing food." This was the woman with whom he remembered spending holidays with his family in Firebaugh, Calif., and Fresno, Calif., after Patricia and her late husband moved there.

"I mean, she was a huge, huge supporter of myself," Allen said. "She went to all the high school games and she made a few NFL games. It's going to (stink) going on without her for sure.

"I wish I could have been there with my family and give them all hugs, but it is what it is. She'll be greatly missed and never forgotten, for sure."

Patricia's memory isn't only being embraced by her famous grandson and the rest of the Allen family.

In typical fashion, Bills fans and the Western New York community wrapped their giant arms of generosity around her memory as well. They did it by making donations of $17 to Buffalo's Oishei Children's Hospital, because of the charitable connection it has had with Allen since he joined the Bills in 2018.

Josh Allen showed off a more personal side after the unexpected passing of his grandmother, Patricia, whom Allen affectionately called "Grammy." (Harry Scull Jr./Buffalo News)

As of Wednesday evening, Oishei reported the total surpassed $335,000 from more than 17,000 donors. The emotions that have been stirring in the Allen family since the weekend have only intensified with that unbridled outpouring of support.

"Words can't really describe how I feel, how my family feels," Allen said. "Every time I call my parents and let them know the new number, they just start bawling all over again. And to know that people care and that so much good is coming out of a tough situation, it means the world to myself, it means the world to my family.

"It just shows how this Bills community and this Buffalo community rally around each other and that's what they've been known for and that's what they're still known for. I mean, I can't thank everybody who supported and donated, I can't thank them enough. It's overwhelming, for sure, but so much good is coming out of such a tough situation that you can't help but smile at it.

"It's unbelievable."

The same can be said for the way Allen handled himself after receiving the news Saturday that he said left him in shock and disbelief. He revealed that his parents initially didn't want to tell him of his grandmother's passing until after the game so as to not "burden me with a heavy heart."

Once they let him know, Allen said he never gave any thought to not playing against the Seahawks. He said that "Grammy" would have wanted him to play "and to play how I usually play, the fun that I have out there and the sense of pride I have when I put on that uniform and I represent the Buffalo Bills and represent my family. That's all I kept telling myself was that I was doing this for her and I knew she was with me on the field."

Of course, after doing his best to "put on a brave face" and keep "a cool head," Allen did far more than just play. He equaled a season and career high with 415 passing yards, three touchdowns through the air and one rushing. Besides AFC Offensive Player of the Week recognition, Allen also was named the FedEx Air NFL Player of the Week.

That was all well and good, but none of those accolades could top the sheer elation of having the sort of game that would have brought some of the loudest cheers from "Grammy."

"To go out there and play for her and to do it in her honor, all my family was all together watching, I mean, I don't think it could have been a better tribute," Allen said. "She was a huge Bills fan."

A few times during Sunday's game, Allen would look up and point his finger to sky. It was his way of letting "Grammy" know that she was in his heart with every completion and touchdown.

"I had some words for her," he said. "It was a long 24 hours."

After the game, Allen called his family. They did what families do when they lose a loved one. They cried together.

"But (his mother and father) both said, 'She's got the best seat in house, her and Papa do,'" Allen said. "It was pretty surreal. It was a special moment for myself and my family."

Not many others outside of the Allen family were aware of his grandmother's death before or during the game. Allen said it was a small group that included coach Sean McDermott, offensive coordinator Brian Daboll and "a couple guys in the quarterback room."

"Honestly, I think few guys didn't really know what was going on even after the game when I kind of spoke to everybody," Allen said. "But just talking with some of the guys who had been through situations like mine, a guy like Mario Addison (who lost his brother last year) coming up to me, just giving me a big hug and letting me know like, 'We're going to get through this together.'"

At that moment, it wasn't a defensive end embracing a quarterback. It was brother hugging a grandson and sharing a bond called grief. ∎

Bills fans and the Western New York community responded with a huge level of support for the Allen family, donating hundreds of thousands of dollars to Buffalo's Oishei Children's Hospital in Patricia Allen's memory. (Harry Scull Jr./ Buffalo News)

A HELPING HAND

Why an 11-Year-Old's Name is Inscribed in Allen's Cleats

By Jay Skurski | December 12, 2020

Bills quarterback Josh Allen got some help in designing his cleats for Sunday's game against the Pittsburgh Steelers from Tom Low, an 11-year-old from South Buffalo.

Low, who attends City Honors, spent 18 days last summer at Oishei Children's Hospital after an infection in his eye ended up traveling to his brain, necessitating two surgeries.

Allen, who works closely with the hospital, bonded with Low when they discussed the release of the third season of "Stranger Things" on Netflix.

So when the quarterback needed some help with the design process for the NFL's "My Cause, My Cleats campaign," he asked his buddy.

During a video call Friday, Allen showed Low the finished product.

"I've got some really cool things to show you, you ready for them? Your design, it came out fantastic," Allen told Low. "I'm going to have the coolest cleats on the field come Sunday, I promise you that."

Allen's white Nikes feature green, yellow and red stripes on the exterior. Low's name is on the interior of both shoes. Allen's favorite part is found on the back, which makes sense after Low explained how he came up with the design.

"I looked up some pictures online of Children's Hospital and the main thing I noticed was on the sides, they have those rainbow stripes, so I got the idea to do those stripes like that," he said. "On the back you see there are angel wings and I said to put those because I thought the nurses were like angels there because they are so nice and caring."

"So that's why these cleats are so special to me," Allen told Low. "It is the coolest pair of cleats that I'm going to put on my feet. I can't wait to wear them. I just can't stop looking at them. I really can't. All my teammates are so jealous, too. You did such a good job, buddy."

Getting to showcase all the amazing work the doctors, nurses and staff at the hospital on a national stage is special for Allen.

Bills fans donated more than $700,000 to Oishei in memory of Allen's grandmother, Patricia, in the aftermath of her death last month, with some of the proceeds being used for the Patricia Allen Pediatric Recovery Wing on the hospital's sports-themed 10th floor.

"I'm not just representing the hospital. I'm representing the nurses who work there. That's why we've got the angel wings on the back like Tom said," he said. "The doctors who work there. The patients who go there and their families that have to spend time there. These cleats represent all that. Obviously, I get to donate these after and the proceeds go straight to Oishei. I couldn't think of a better cause and better way to represent what I care about than to wear them on my feet on a nationally televised game."

Before Allen and Low finished their conversation Friday, the quarterback had one last piece of advice.

"Make sure you do your homework," he said, to which Low said he certainly would. ∎

Josh Allen has become a hero to Bills fans on and off the field, complementing his tremendous play with a compassionate persona and strong connection to the community. (Harry Scull Jr./Buffalo News)

'WON NOT DONE'

AFC East Title Shirt is Nice, But Allen Wants Super Bowl Swag

By Jason Wolf | December 20, 2020

Josh Allen executed a near-perfect Statue of Liberty play, throwing the fake pass with his right arm while handing the ball behind his back to Devin Singletary, who crossed the goal line, only to have the touchdown negated by a penalty.

It was the first of three consecutive flags against the Bills, a trio of miscues that set up first-and-goal at the 30-yard line.

They were just making things interesting.

Moments later, Allen whipped a 22-yard touchdown pass to Jake Kumerow, the NFL record-tying 13th player to catch a touchdown for the Bills this season, as Buffalo completed its march to the AFC East throne, clinching its first division championship in a quarter century by thrashing the Denver Broncos 48-19 on national television Saturday at Empower Field at Mile High.

The Bills last won the division title in 1995.

Allen was born in 1996.

"It's great that we're able to do it for the first time in 25 years," Allen said. "To be the team and to be the quarterback of the team that does it obviously feels really good. At the same time, that's not our main goal. We set out to do this in order to give us the chance to do what we really want to do, and that's to win Super Bowl championships."

At least that was what Allen told reporters. In a video of the postgame locker room celebration posted by the Bills on social media, a more fiery Allen had his teammates around him, all wearing division championships shirts and hats, and yelled, "This hat and this shirt is fine and dandy, but I want the one that says (expletive) Super Bowl champions."

But this accomplishment, for this franchise, for this fanbase, is extraordinary.

The Bills (11-3) have started 22 different quarterbacks, including Jim Kelly, since last winning the division. And the kid from Firebaugh, Calif., finally led them out of the desert, in his third year as a pro, with two games remaining in the regular season.

Allen accounted for four touchdowns against the Broncos (5-9). He completed 28 of 40 passes for 359 yards and two touchdowns, hitting tight end Dawson Knox and Kumerow, the former practice squad receiver, in the end zone. He also rushed for 33 yards and two scores, delivering a division championship that this week felt like an inevitability.

The buildup mounted for days on social media, with #BillsMafia posting photos of small children wearing their parents' Kelly jerseys, of vintage Starter jackets and Christmas ornaments, of family and friends who sadly didn't live to see this day.

The Bills finished the 1995 regular season with a 10-6 record, edging the 9-7 Indianapolis Colts and 9-7 Miami Dolphins for the division title, years before realignment. They've already surpassed that win total on the way to a third playoff appearance in four seasons.

"This is just a blessing from God," Bills coach Sean McDermott said. "Honestly, man, I'm just humbled to be a part of it. I think it's so cool when the guys that are so young can tie into the past, and they know those early '90s (teams), they see the banners hanging in our facility every day that are there. ... And even before those teams. And I should thank, also, the guys that have supported us in so many ways from those teams.

"Coach (Marv) Levy, Jim Kelly, Thurman (Thomas), Steve Tasker, Cornelius Bennett, Bruce Smith, Darryl

Josh Allen completed 28 passes for 359 yards and two touchdowns in Buffalo's win in Denver. (Associated Press)

Talley. All those guys, man. They live and die with us… I also feel a responsibility – I think all of our players do, as well – a responsibility to do things the right way for those guys, as well, because they started this years ago."

Allen and Stefon Diggs are etching their names alongside those greats.

Diggs finished with 11 catches on 13 targets for 147 yards, all game highs. He leads the NFL with a franchise-record 111 catches and 1,314 receiving yards this season.

The fans' fervor rose to a crescendo on social media as Allen put on a show, rewriting the Bills' record book against a Broncos secondary ravaged by injuries and suspension.

Allen's touchdown pass to Kumerow was his 30th of the season, passing a milestone previously attained only by Kelly, who tossed 33 scores in 1991. That record could fall next week, when the Bills try to sweep the New England Patriots for the first time since 1999, on Monday Night Football.

Allen has thrown for at least 300 yards in seven games this season, tying a franchise record set by Drew Bledsoe in 2002. He also joined Bledsoe as the only quarterbacks in franchise history to pass for 4,000 yards in a season. He also finished with with a passer rating above 100 for the seventh time this season, another franchise record.

And the fireworks weren't limited to the air.

Allen's second rushing touchdown of the game was the 25th of his career, tying the franchise record set by Jack Kemp.

He's the second player in NFL history with at least eight rushing touchdowns and 30 passing touchdowns in a season, joining Cam Newton in 2015.

"It's hard to even be impressed now," wide receiver Cole Beasley said, shrugging off Allen's dominant performance. "It's expected."

McDermott laughed and agreed.

"He just continues to get better, and I think that's the cool part about it," McDermott said. "He's so humble. He's a great teammate. And I'm extremely proud of him. I don't take it for granted. Quarterbacks that can play at that level are hard to find, and (general manager) Brandon (Beane) did a phenomenal job. Give Coach (Brian) Daboll, the offensive staff (credit). And again

we're coming together as a team, now, too."

Bills offensive lineman Jon Feliciano said this game was personal for Allen, who played his college ball in Laramie, Wyoming, just 130 miles north of Denver, considering the Broncos didn't select him with the fifth pick in the 2018 draft.

"He might not say it, but he definitely still remembers that," Feliciano said.

Allen, drafted seventh overall, took a moment to consider a similar question.

"I'm where I'm supposed to be," he said.

Allen's 55-yard pass to Diggs in the third quarter was the longest of the season.

There is no debate about whether the Bills or Minnesota Vikings won the trade.

Diggs and Beasley, who had eight catches for 112 yards, became the first Bills duo to surpass 100 receiving yards in a game since 2010.

Allen, Singletary and Zack Moss combined to roll up 182 rushing yards and three touchdowns on 24 carries, an average of 7.6 yards per touch.

And even the defense scored, with Jerry Hughes, the longest-tenured member of the Bills, scooping a fumble caused by Tre'Davious White and dancing 21 yards into the end zone.

The Bills were plagued by a late spate of injuries, an obvious concern. Diggs was taken to the locker room with a foot issue in the fourth quarter but returned to the sideline. White suffered a stinger. Levi Wallace hurt an ankle. A.J. Epenesa was evaluated for a head injury. Andre Roberts hurt his back. McDermott was unable to provide status updates immediately after the contest.

But there are three weeks to heal and prepare to host a playoff game.

"Our shirts say, 'WON NOT DONE,'" Allen said, "so everything's still in front of us and this just gives us an opportunity to give us a shot, and that's all we can ask for."

Matt Barkley replaced Allen with 1:51 remaining in the fourth quarter, with no need to subject the franchise quarterback to further risk. He handed off to Singletary, who raced 51 yards for a touchdown, the longest of his career.

This time, it counted. ■

Josh Allen rushed for two touchdowns against the Broncos. His 25 career rushing TDs tied Jack Kemp for the Bills' franchise record. (Associated Press)

NOT TOO WILD

Mature, Composed Allen Leads Bills to First Playoff Win Since '95

By Vic Carucci | January 9, 2021

This was the kind of game that demanded composure and maturity.

It was, to the very end, a grind. It was as much, if not more, about survival than triumph.

A year ago, at Houston, the Buffalo Bills allowed themselves to come apart and the result was a sudden and crushing end to the postseason in the AFC wild-card round. On Saturday at Bills Stadium, they kept it together and escaped with a 27-24 wild-card victory against the Indianapolis Colts for their first playoff win since 1995.

What was the difference?

"I think just leadership, probably more than anything," coach Sean McDermott told reporters after his first playoff victory as a head coach after going 0-2 in the postseason since arriving in Buffalo in 2017. "Maturity, professionalism. Yeah, that's what comes to mind more than anything else."

And Josh Allen, more than any player on the team, carried the burden of having to show those traits after his failure to do so did the most to cause the Bills to blow a 16-point lead on the way to a 22-19 overtime loss against the Texans.

On Saturday, he showed the necessary poise that allowed the Bills to not let the game slip away as the Colts trimmed a 14-point deficit to three with about six minutes remaining in the fourth quarter. The defense came up big, with Micah Hyde's knockdown of a Philip Rivers Hail Mary pass as time expired and a huge goal-line stand in the first half, as did a pair of rookies: Gabe Davis, with clutch catches, and Tyler Bass, with clutch kicking.

But nowhere was the spotlight brighter than on Allen.

After failing to throw for a touchdown and completing only 52% of his throws in his playoff debut against Houston, he bounced back in a big way by mostly maintaining his dominant 2020 form. In allowing the Bills to snap a five-game wild-card losing streak that dated to 1996, Allen passed for 324 yards and two touchdowns, with no interceptions, for a passer rating of 121.6. He also was the Bills' leading rusher with 54 yards and a TD on 11 carries.

Allen became the only NFL player ever to throw for 300-plus yards, have a 70-plus completion percentage and rush for 50-plus yards in a playoff game.

For Allen, who produced the Bills' fifth 300-plus-yard playoff passing performance all-time and first since Doug Flutie's 360 at Miami in 1999, it came down to maintaining awareness of the flow of the game.

"Understanding not to press, not to do too much. That was the only thing that was on my mind," Allen told reporters. "I was staying calm on the sideline. I understood there was still a lot of game left. I was just trying to reiterate that to my teammates, trying to be that leader by example, not trying to get too worked up over the small things."

The Bills will need more of the same next weekend at Bills Stadium, when they play their first divisional-round game since '95. The opponent depends on the outcome of Sunday night's game between the Pittsburgh Steelers and Cleveland Browns. If the Steelers win, they will face the Bills. If the Browns win, the Bills will face the winner of Sunday's game between the Baltimore Ravens and Tennessee Titans.

The Colts' defense was stout in the first half, limiting opportunities for Stefon Diggs and Cole Beasley. But Allen got them going in the second half, with Diggs

Josh Allen passed for 324 yards and two touchdowns in the Bills' AFC wild-card victory over the Indianapolis Colts. (Harry Scull Jr./Buffalo News)

catching a 35-yard touchdown pass to give the Bills a 24-10 lead early in the fourth quarter. Diggs finished with six receptions for 128 yards, Beasley had seven for 57 yards, and Davis had four for 85 yards.

Allen's effectiveness on his feet wasn't limited to the yards he gained. In the first quarter, with the Bills at the Colts' 3-yard line, Allen began running, but with defenders closing in on him in the backfield, he threw a pass while falling to his right and connected with Dawson Knox for a touchdown to make it 7-3.

The Colts answered with a 1-yard Jonathan Taylor touchdown run. But the game turned late in the first half when the Bills staged a goal-line stand, stopping the Colts on fourth down from the Buffalo 4, and proceeded to drive 96 yards to a five-yard Allen touchdown run. That put the Bills in front, 14-10. They never trailed the rest of the way, even if there were some anxious moments in the final minutes.

"I'm still kicking myself for a couple plays," Allen said.

Perhaps the biggest was when Allen, while being sacked for a 14-yard loss, fought to stay upright and wound up losing the ball. Offensive tackle Daryl Williams recovered, but the mistake pushed the Bills back to their 43. Rather than being in position to expand their lead and minimize the chances of the Colts potentially kicking a tying field goal or scoring a go-ahead touchdown, the Bills were forced to punt, giving Indianapolis the ball at its 14 with 2:30 left.

The Bills then had to sweat out the remaining time.

Allen relayed a conversation he had with offensive coordinator Brian Daboll after the game, as the Bills look to the next round.

"He said, 'This is playoff football. You've got to forget about it, you've got to focus on next week. It doesn't matter what we did. Back to 0-0. Whoever we're going to face, they're 0-0 coming into our house and we've got to prepare and get ready to go,'" Allen said. "Being in that situation we were in last year, taking that experience, understanding that these drives that we have are precious, but it's not the end of the world if we don't get things going right away.

"That's a heck of a football team we just played, make no mistake about it. They came prepared and hungry. They started off with a bang and it took us a second to adjust and catch up to what they were doing."

The Colts' talented defensive front managed to generate steady pressure on Allen, who was sacked twice and hit a half-dozen times. Running backs Zack Moss, before suffering what reportedly is feared to be a season-ending injury, and Devin Singletary each had 21 yards on a combined 10 carries.

"They did a good job of taking away the run, for one," Allen said. "A couple of third downs, third-and-shorts; we've got to find a way to convert on those. They're long, they're fast, side to side. Those linebackers are really good. They really squeeze on some windows extremely fast, get their hands up and make it tougher for the quarterback in the throwing lanes."

A year ago, the sort of challenges the Bills faced from the Colts could have easily caused them to unravel. As with the Texans' Deshaun Watson, the Colts had a quarterback delivering big plays of his own in Rivers, who threw for 309 yards and two TDs.

However, the meltdown didn't happen Saturday. Credit the greater maturity Allen and his teammates have gained in a year, and what they have seen repeatedly from Allen in an MVP-caliber season. "Same old Josh," guard Jon Feliciano said.

"It was one of those things where there was no panic, but there was definitely a sense of urgency," center Mitch Morse added. "When it comes to situations like that, we understand what we need to do. I think, for us, when things don't go our way as a team or as an offense, it's tough. Emotions are amplified in the playoffs. I thought we had a lot of good stuff there and we learned a lot. Kudos to the guys for kind of bouncing back and putting together a good game."

Kudos, too, to an organizational mindset that starts at the top.

"We understand that whatever's going on in the game, we feel like we've got a chance," Allen said. "That's just based on how we play, how we trust one another, how we care for one another, how we practice. Just the foundation that's been set up by our front office and Terry and Kim (Pegula). It is a family like atmosphere here and we want to do everything in our power not to let each other down." ■

In the win over the Colts, Josh Allen became the only NFL player ever to throw for 300-plus yards, have a 70-plus completion percentage and rush for 50-plus yards in a playoff game. (Harry Scull Jr./Buffalo News)

WRITING HISTORY

Bills Advance Despite Little Success on the Ground

By Jason Wolf | January 17, 2021

Who needs a running game? Not the Buffalo Bills.

The Bills rushed for just 32 yards on 16 attempts and called a single running play in the first half of their 17-3 victory against the Baltimore Ravens on Saturday night in wind-whipped Orchard Park, but nevertheless advanced to the AFC championship game for the first time since the 1993 season after a game-changing 101-yard interception return for a touchdown by cornerback Taron Johnson.

"It's going to take everybody moving forward," quarterback Josh Allen said. "We understand that. We can't just rely on one guy to do their job."

Allen completed 23 of 37 pass attempts for 206 yards and a touchdown. He added three rushing yards on seven carries.

With both kickers missing field goals and passes sailing in the icy wind, the Bills didn't even bother to run the football for most of the game against the Ravens, deciding they were incapable of executing much in the way of a ground attack.

Buffalo called 26 offensive plays in the first half. One was a called run. It came with 3:07 remaining. Devin Singletary managed three yards. (The Bills' other two rushes in the first half were a four-yard scramble by Allen and a kneel down to send the teams into the locker room.)

The performance resulted in a 3-3 tie at halftime and at least a slight recalibration at intermission.

"The wind was an ordeal. It was definitely an ordeal," center Mitch Morse said. "So for us it was just trying to keep it to maybe shallow routes, getting out the ball quicker, making yards after catch and for us trying to establish a little bit of a run game."

Buffalo's offense had the ball just once in the third quarter, but the Bills scored 14 points after finally getting the running game involved on a long touchdown drive and Johnson's historic interception return, which tied for the longest in NFL postseason history.

Singletary finished with 25 rushing yards on seven carries. T.J. Yeldon had four yards on two carries.

Buffalo called more running plays on its touchdown drive to begin the second half than it did in the first 30 minutes of the game.

The Bills traveled 66 yards in 11 plays and 5:31, by far the team's longest and most successful drive of the game, in part because they got the ground game going.

Singletary rushed for 20 yards on three carries before Allen capped the drive with a three-yard touchdown pass to Stefon Diggs, providing the Bills with a 10-3 lead with 9 1/2 minutes remaining in the third quarter.

"I think overall we did expect to run the ball a little bit more than we did," Bills coach Sean McDermott said. "I think it just got away from us, but they are a good,

Josh Allen fires a touchdown pass to wide receiver Stefon Diggs during the third quarter of the Bills' AFC divisional playoff game against the Baltimore Ravens. The score gave the Bills a 10–3 lead. (Harry Scull Jr./Buffalo News)

stout front. They're big, strong, long up front. And so I thought we did come out in the second half and establish some rhythm there."

The Ravens owned the top-rated rushing attack in the NFL after averaging nearly 192 yards on the ground this season. But the prolific rushing attack couldn't save Baltimore once it trailed Buffalo by double digits.

Johnson's coast-to-coast score provided the Bills with a 17-3 lead, and the 14-point swing, coupled with a head injury to Ravens quarterback Lamar Jackson that knocked him out of the game on the final play of the third quarter, all but secured the victory.

But even at that point the Bills continued throwing the ball, unable or unwilling to grind out the victory on the ground.

In three scoreless possessions, including one that began on the Baltimore 29-yard line, Singletary managed two yards on three carries and Yeldon had four yards on two carries.

The Ravens allowed an average of 4.6 yards per carry this season, but last week held two-time rushing champ Derrick Henry to just 40 yards on 18 carries.

Buffalo had success with a similar pass-heavy game plan in Week 9 against the Seattle Seahawks, when Allen completed 31 of 38 passes for 415 yards and three touchdowns. He also rushed seven times for 14 yards and a score. Zack Moss rushed nine times for 18 yards and a touchdown, Singletary rushed twice for 1 yard and Isaiah McKenzie added a carry. It was 69 degrees at kickoff that day.

It was 30 degrees with a swirling wind against the Ravens.

And the Bills were without Moss, who's out for the rest of the postseason because of an ankle injury.

When the Bills' final drive of the first half sputtered at midfield after another incomplete pass, the Ravens fielded a punt and took over at their own 27-yard line with 1:03 remaining and one timeout.

It was enough time to put their only points on the board.

Jackson connected with a wide-open Marquise Brown on a wobbly pass that picked up 30 yards to the Buffalo 35, and Justin Tucker hit a 34-yard field goal to tie the score at 3-3 with 4 seconds remaining in the first half.

Tucker had missed two field goals already. A 41-yard attempt in the first quarter bounced off the left upright. A 46-yard attempt in the second quarter bounced off the right upright.

Tucker had never missed multiple field goals from inside 50 yards in the same game. He was 11 for 11 on field goals from inside 50 yards in his playoff career.

Bills rookie Tyler Bass was 1 for 3. He knocked one through from 28 yards in the first quarter after the Bills took over at the Baltimore 38 following a shanked punt.

He also missed from 43 yards in the second quarter and 44 yards in the fourth.

Ravens quarterback Tyler Huntley, an undrafted rookie free agent who replaced Jackson, sailed a potential touchdown pass over Brown on fourth down midway through the fourth quarter.

"It's only going to get tougher from here," Allen said. "We're ready for it. We're just excited for an opportunity to play next week." ■

In a game in which the Bills rushed for just 32 yards, Josh Allen completed 23 of 37 pass attempts for 206 yards to lead the Bills to victory. (James P. McCoy/Buffalo News)

PUTTING IN THE WORK

How Allen Improved His Accuracy

By Vic Carucci | January 19, 2021

Accurate passing can't be coached. Either you have it or you don't. And if you weren't an accurate passer in college, you aren't going to become one in the NFL.

How often have we heard that since the runup to the 2018 NFL draft?

Josh Allen's detractors put it at the top of the reasons that he wasn't worthy of the seventh overall choice the Buffalo Bills used to select him. It was spoken with such authority and conviction, as if it were gospel handed down from the football gods.

There's just one problem. In the case of Allen, it has proved false.

A 13-3 Bills season highlighted by the team's first AFC East championship in 25 years, its most victories in a season since 1991 and a No. 2 playoff seed doesn't happen without the dynamic play of Allen. He has set single season franchise records for passing yards (4,544), touchdown passes (37), completions (396), 300-yard passing games (eight) and total yards (4,987, including 12 receiving).

But those achievements wouldn't be possible without the most defining stat of Allen's rise to elite status: His career-high completion percentage of 69.2, which ranks fourth in the NFL.

Allen's adjusted completion percentage, which takes into account spikes, throwaways and throws impacted by hits, rose from 71.2% in 2019 to 79.2%, according to Pro Football Focus.

Coming three seasons after a career at Wyoming, where he completed 56.2% of his throws, it makes a solid argument that a quarterback can, in fact, become significantly more accurate as a pro.

"I have seen a real improvement in his accuracy," Troy Aikman, Hall of Fame quarterback and lead NFL game analyst for Fox Sports, told The Buffalo News by phone. "And it's a real credit to his work ethic. I mean, he has clearly worked really hard at it. … My years as a player and now as a broadcaster, he is one of the few that I can think of that has shown noticeable improvement in that area."

Aikman readily acknowledges he was an Allen detractor in 2018. While he's willing to make an exception for Allen, Aikman unapologetically subscribes to the logic that inaccurate passers in college tend to stay that way in the NFL. Aikman's completion percentage in college was 63.3, helped greatly by his transfer from Oklahoma and its Wishbone offense, and he had a completion percentage of 61.5 in a Hall of Fame career.

"I was accurate as a passer and I just I feel you either have an ability to put a ball where you want to or you don't," Aikman said. "And that was a real concern, I guess, of Josh coming out. Heck, I saw him miss 10-yard throws. And not even close. And you'd say, 'Wow!' When I was at his pro day, I was standing right behind him and I happened to be next to Mike Shula (when he was offensive coordinator of the New York Giants). He threw a ball, it had to be 85 yards in the air. I've never seen a

Josh Allen throws a pass during the Bills' Jan. 3, 2021, win over the Miami Dolphins. (Harry Scull Jr./Buffalo News)

Josh Allen scrambles to evade Dolphins linebacker Shaq Lawson. Allen's improved understanding of opposing defenses was key in his improvement in 2021. (James P. McCoy/Buffalo News)

ball travel like that. He overthrew the receiver and it was the darndest thing I've ever seen.

"When people start talking about strong arms and this and that, I saw Brett Favre launch one about 78 yards one time. I've never seen anyone with an arm like Josh Allen's. Now, where does that get you? Well, not very far. I mean, it helps you with a Hail Mary if you're on your own 20-yard line, but other than that ...

"I'm asked a lot, 'Hey, what do you think the most important quality is for a quarterback?' I have always said it's accuracy, because you can have all of the other things – great leadership, great toughness, arm strength, smart – and it just doesn't matter. If you can't throw a football where you want to throw it, then what good are you?"

After throwing for 417 yards and four touchdowns – with three passes of 46 or more yards and seven completions in eight attempts of 20-plus yards – in a 31-28 victory at Miami on Sept. 20, Allen was asked if all the talk about his lack of long-ball accuracy could be put to rest.

"I'm asking you," said Allen, who was among the worst in the league in 2019 in 20-plus-yard throws with a 30.9% completion rate, per Pro Football Focus.

He would provide an answer to that question as he put together an MVP-caliber season. That deep-ball figure has mushroomed to 47.9% this year on almost the same number of attempts, and Allen's improvement hasn't just come on longer throws.

"It seems like Josh is a little bit more composed and comfortable in stepping up in the pocket," said Broncos safety Justin Simmons before Allen completed 70% of his passes for 359 yards in a December win against Denver. "He's making accurate throws all across the field."

'Worked his butt off'

When Allen's completion percentage dipped from 56.2% in college to 52.8% in his rookie year, a chorus of "I told you so" rang out. It didn't get all that much quieter when the number climbed to a modest 58.8% in 2019.

After completing only 52.2% of his passes in a

Josh Allen and Bills free safety Jordan Poyer have some fun before a game at Bills Stadium. (Harry Scull Jr./Buffalo News)

forgettable performance in the Bills' wild-card playoff loss at Houston, Allen and his coaches knew there was plenty of work to be done. Even in an offseason when the pandemic wiped out practices at team facilities, he managed to invest enough time on his own, including his annual sessions in Southern California with personal quarterback coach Jordan Palmer, to sufficiently address his throwing mechanics.

One component of his work with Palmer was having his mechanics digitally mapped, a process that allowed Allen to better understand how throwing motion correlates to accuracy and power. As he explained early last month while appearing on "The Pat McAfee Show," the mapping showed "what was firing … (it is supposed to be) my hips, then my torso, then your elbow and your hand firing. But my hand and elbow were firing near before my hips were. I wasn't really incorporating any part of my legs in my motion."

"Being able to add my hips and make that as consistent as possible and try to slow everything else

down up top and use my hand as the leverage for the speed and the accuracy has changed a lot of things," Allen said. "The accuracy has gone up, but it's actually added some mph to my throwing power, too. It's been a pretty cool process. … It was like a wake-up call. It was like, 'OK, maybe I should try to incorporate a few clubs into my bag and try to hit that 60 degrees.' It's funny that I use golf as that metaphor because I've actually learned a lot of my throwing from my swing in golf."

Additionally, in focusing on deep-ball accuracy, Palmer put Allen and his other clients through drills that had them throwing to receivers at the top of a hill or stadium bleachers. They had to get the ball to rotate and drop down, despite the target being 15 to 20 yards above them.

"What it does is it exaggerates the shoulder tilt and your spine tilting back," Palmer told The News in January. "And then we bring them down the stands. You do that over a period of a month or so and it's kind of like you develop both sides of the spectrum, both extremes. Too high and not high enough."

Passing from the bottom of an incline "kind of forces you to throw the ball with arc over the top and drop it in instead of trying to drive it," Bills quarterbacks coach Ken Dorsey told The News. "It just forces you to get elevation on the throw, and it gives you a little bit more margin of error when you do that."

Allen also followed the guidance he received via video calls with Dorsey and offensive coordinator Brian Daboll. Their instruction continued in-person once the NFL allowed training camps to open.

Aikman and others who know what it takes to excel as a quarterback admire the amount of time and effort Allen invested to improve his passing skills.

"I think he worked his butt off," former NFL quarterback and CBS game analyst Rich Gannon told The News. "The feet are a big thing. I know he's talked a lot about being in balance in the throws, not overstriding. He's worked a lot on that. I think he's worked on his release mechanics. I think he's done a lot of technical work and fundamental work on that.

"I just think the fact that he's taken it to another level where, in the offseason he's going out to California, spending his own money to work on some of those core fundamentals and techniques, all of that shows. He's worked on core strength. I think he's also worked a lot on a whole routine to get himself warmed up before he throws every day and cool down, taking care of his arm, which guys didn't do 15 years ago.

"I think a lot of the credit has to go to Brian Daboll and the coaching staff; they've done a really good job with him. But I think a lot of credit goes to the kid. I had a conversation with him in one of our production meetings and believe me, he is well aware, as are all quarterbacks, what the talk on the street is about him. He's heard the criticism."

The addition of Stefon Diggs has done wonders to boost Allen's production in all areas. Besides Diggs' ability to separate from defenders, his presence has helped allow other receivers to have more room to operate. And when they have more room, Allen has a greater chance of getting them the ball consistently.

The Bills have thrown more passes this season, with Allen's percentage of deep attempts decreasing as the intermediate passing game has opened up. Cole Beasley, who generally operates on underneath routes, is having a career year with personal bests in targets (107), receptions (82) and yards (967).

In passes that travel to 10 to 20 yards, Allen has upped his completion percentage from 61.7% to 64.2%, moving from 58 of 94 last year to 79 of 123 this year.

"Everyone knows he has the arm," the Broncos' Simmons said, "not to mention the additional weapon they got with Diggs, he's an elite receiver."

Allen's game experience has also paid large dividends.

"When he walked to the line of scrimmage against the Ravens that first game of his rookie year, there was a million things coming at him," Gannon said. "And it all happened so fast. Now, all of a sudden, he's seeing the corner's heels at 10 yards on one side; the other guy's at eight. He's seeing the safety, who's usually three yards outside the numbers and now and he's down in the box area. He starts seeing the Will linebacker who's bossed a little bit (sliding to the strong side).

"Not only that, but he's starting to see things on the offensive side of the ball. Cole Beasley's split is supposed to be three yards from the tackle; now he's five yards. Little tips and reminders. Now you're an air traffic controller. He's still not quite there yet, but, man, he's made big progress. I think he's the most improved player in the league this year. And that's saying a lot because, in my opinion, he was trending in the right direction last year."

'Understanding everything'

Gannon calls himself a "great example" of a QB who elevated his completion percentage during the course of his career. He went from 33.3 in 1987, as a rookie with the Minnesota Vikings, to 59.6 by his fifth season. Gannon improved to 63.6 in 1995, his first year with the Kansas City Chiefs, and hit a career-high 67.6 in 2002 with the Oakland Raiders, winning NFL MVP honors and leading his team to the Super Bowl.

He believes the reason for his improvement applies to Allen and all quarterbacks.

"One is a better understanding of everything, and it starts with protections," Gannon said. "When you start understanding the protections, you start understanding the strength of the protection, the weakness, where you're vulnerable, who's hot, who's not, where you have to change the protection, where you have to speed up the drop, all those type of things help you. The second thing is understanding coverages and fronts. If it's an under front, and the safety's in a strike position, there's a good chance there's going to be some kind of blitz. Now I've got some answers in my toolbox for that. I can audible the protection, I can sight-adjust, I can hand-signal the receiver, I can do all these different things.

"I think he's got a better understanding of the why. Why is Daboll calling this particular play in this situation in the game, the down and distance and score? Because he's expecting blitz or he's expecting two-deep coverage or he's expecting man-to-man. All those things begin to factor into your ability to be more accurate, because you're more decisive, you have better anticipation.

"You watched him early in his career, he has such a strong arm, but he had to see the guy clearly coming out of the break, he had to see the guy clearly have some separation. Now you watch him, and he's throwing the ball before these guys are out of the break a lot of times because he trusts the receivers. He understands the importance of timing and rhythm in the passing game. His feet have gotten better in the pocket. You watch him, whether he's in the gun or he's working under the center, he's become a much better play-action passer."

It's fair to say that at least some of Allen's accuracy issues have been circumstantial. He grew up in Firebaugh, Calif., which is hardly a hotbed for quarterbacks. Allen wasn't building up his resume for college recruiters by attending prestigious passing camps. He wasn't on anyone's recruiting hot list.

As a member of the Firebaugh junior varsity team in 2011, Allen had a completion percentage of 59.5. It was 50.8% and 57.4% in his two seasons on the varsity.

"It was really just him and his high school coach probably working on it," Dorsey said. "Then he goes to junior college for a couple years (Reedley, where his completion percentage dipped to 49). And then he goes to Wyoming for a couple years. So, it's not like he was in one place for like four or five years with the same coaching staff in college, to where they could really home in on things or anything like that."

There are other examples, though not many, of top-level NFL quarterbacks improving completion percentage from the beginning of their careers.

Steve Young went from 52.2% in 1985, his first year with the San Francisco 49ers when he made five starts while backing up fellow Hall of Famer Joe Montana, to 69.6% in 1989 when he made three starts to 66.7% in 1992 when he went 12-2 as a starter.

The Saints' Drew Brees jumped from 57.6% in 2003, his third NFL season with the San Diego Chargers, to 65.5% a year later, his next-to-last season with the Chargers.

The common thread is an exceptional work ethic.

"I think, number one, it starts with the individual and the type of guy you're dealing with," Dorsey said. "Is he willing to put in extra time? Is he willing to basically sacrifice a lot of stuff to really focus on his job, his profession? And Josh is really willing to do that in the offseason and in-season, whether it's drill work, whether it's extra throwing, whether it's watching tape. I think the most important thing is you've got a guy who is hungry to improve and eager to learn and work on his craft. A part of that is just really focusing on the mechanics, building a great base of fundamentals."

Strong base

Allen likes to see his throwing motion through the lens of golf. For Dorsey, the closer sporting comparison is boxing.

"I equate it a lot with a boxer," he said. "If a boxer is standing straight up and he's not moving his feet, he's going to get knocked out. The fight isn't going to last very long. Whereas, if he's playing with a great base and has a solid lower body, generally he's going to give himself a chance. I think it's the same thing with quarterback play. We focus a lot on the lower body and the base mechanics, because very rarely do you play in an NFL football game where you just drop back and you could just sit in the pocket all day and you're throwing seven-on-seven. You're going to have to slide and adjust, you're going to have to move in the pocket and kind of stress yourself and then you have to get back into a throwing position or have to throw a little off-balance.

"When you watch the most successful guys around the league, they have very good lower-body mechanics in their base and that's where you generate a lot of power from and that's where you generate a lot of accuracy from. But we try, as best we can, to replicate that through drill work."

It starts with a good, strong base with good knee-bend and foot movement. "Not letting your feet go dead is the main thing," the coach said.

After that, it's about keeping the shoulders level,

with the front shoulder (the left in the case of a right-handed thrower like Allen) tight to the body to prevent it from rising.

"When you throw an intermediate or short ball, if your front shoulder's raised, in order to throw it accurately, you've got to bring it back down to level so the ball doesn't sail on you. Obviously, that's something he worked on as well," Dorsey said. "Naturally, there's going to be some throws where it elevates because you're putting arc on the ball and throwing it over the top. So sometimes there are those throws where you elevate the shoulder, but for the most part, you want good level and staying tight."

Allen came to recognize how vital good footwork was to his game when he began training with Palmer before the 2018 draft.

"I had a problem with a long front step and that was causing my elbow to drop, and it was throwing off the entire sequence within the hip and the shoulder and the arm coming through," Allen told The News during his rookie training camp. "So when I keep that steady and I can take a small front stride and get (the left foot) down, my lead step, as fast as possible, the ball comes out quicker, it comes out cleaner, my throwing motion is less violent and that equals more accurate balls."

Step one of the Palmer method is having his clients jump as high as possible multiple times, land and look down.

"And I'll say, 'OK, that is your base. We're going to operate within a couple inches inside or outside of that base,'" Palmer said. "From there, I got to the root of the problem: his feet. He's overstriding. And I go, 'Well, why are you overstriding? Because your base is too narrow. You're putting yourself in a position where you have to overstride. So let's not fix the overstride, let's fix the base.'"

Among the tactics Palmer employed was having Allen wear a resistance band around his ankles while he went through drills. The purpose was twofold: 1. It

helped strengthen Allen's base; 2. It reminded him of the proper distance to maintain between his feet.

"The outside of your butt, your posterior glute, is weak," Palmer said. "So if I put a band around your ankles and have you move around, it's going to burn right away. No matter how big and buff you are, if that's a muscle group that's not being addressed, it's going to burn. They're very thin, light bands, but putting them on, it fires that glute and it strengthens it to where you're strong enough to keep your base right there."

That's the mechanical part of Allen's growth and development.

There's a psychological part, as well, and it hasn't been lost on Allen's teammates.

"It's hard when the keys to the franchise are given to you. That can be daunting, both mentally and physically," center Mitch Morse told reporters after the Bills' 56-26 victory against the Dolphins Sunday. "Josh has just been such a poised competitor this year. He really picked us up when we weren't feeling great and kind of marched us forward.

"When a quarterback walks into the huddle and you can feel his confidence even when things aren't going right, that permeates to the rest of the guys and he does an exceptional job of that and the great quarterbacks do, so we're very fortunate to have him."

As the Bills enter the postseason, they know they have a quarterback who is playing the best football of his life. Nowhere is that more evident than with his elevated accuracy.

It hasn't happened by accident.

"Obviously, we're very happy with the direction we're in and the strides that Josh has made," Dorsey said. "And a lot of that, and I can't reiterate enough, is just the work that he's put into it." ∎

Josh Allen throws a pass from the pocket against the Miami Dolphins. Allen's improved pocket footwork has made him a much better play-action passer. (Harry Scull Jr./Buffalo News)

'HE BELONGS ON THAT STAGE'

Josh Allen's Friends Offer a Glimpse at the QB's Mindset

By Jason Wolf | January 20, 2021

A week after the Buffalo Bills lost to the Houston Texans in the first round of the 2019 NFL playoffs, Josh Allen returned home to Northern California and went golfing with three buddies, Greg Panelli, Dominic DeFrancesco and Nolan Sorensen.

Once the foursome finished their round at Dragonfly Golf Club in Madera, Calif., they went to lunch at the PressBox Sports Grill in northeast Fresno, where they walked into the restaurant in the third quarter of Houston's second-round playoff game against the Kansas City Chiefs at Arrowhead Stadium.

"I won't be over this until we start playing again," Allen told reporters in Buffalo a week earlier, the morning after the Bills blew a 16-point second-half lead and were ousted from the postseason 22-19 in overtime. His anguish was still raw.

But now, a year later, Allen is an NFL MVP candidate and the Bills are preparing to face the reigning Super Bowl champion Chiefs in the AFC championship game in Kansas City.

If you didn't already know, it's Josh Allen's world. We're all just living in it.

And his friends from back home, who have known Allen since high school or earlier, spoke to The Buffalo News to recount one of the most unusual meals they've ever shared:

Panelli: "Josh came back and obviously wanted to get out and clear his head a little bit and then we went to go grab some lunch, and right when we walked in, it was just Chiefs fans everywhere. I remember walking in and just looking over at him watching the game and I could just tell, and he said a couple of times, 'Man, we should be here. We should be here. We should be here.'"

DeFrancesco: "Just knowing how competitive he was growing up, it was really tough sitting there. We were trying to have a good time and watch the game and Josh is just kind of beside himself, because he just knows he shouldn't be with us watching the game. He should be playing in it."

Sorensen: "People didn't even really recognize him at the time. It's just like a lowkey pub. We had Buffalo wings and had a beer and watched the football game after a round of golf."

Panelli: "I remember the waitress looked at his ID and she said, 'Wait a second.' And she looked up at him and then looked back down, and she's like, 'This is – you're the Josh Allen?' And he's like, 'Huh? I don't know what you're talking about.' And that's how Josh is. He'll (mess) around all the time. Always having fun."

DeFrancesco: "Golfing, we're not trying to talk about (the Bills) too much. We were trying to unwind, have a good time on the course."

Sorensen: "It's fun going out there. It's a public course, and we don't really know anyone there. We just go out and have a good time. And it's a longer course, too. Josh can hit the ball about a mile, especially if he plays his little 'butter cut,' as we like to call it, and so he

Josh Allen walks off the field after warming up before the Bills' AFC divisional playoff game against the Baltimore Ravens. (Harry Scull Jr./Buffalo News)

just rears back and lets it fly. Some call it a slice. Some call it a butter cut. Pick your poison."

Panelli: "I definitely won that day. This was the first time (we played last year), so of course his rebuttal was, 'Well you had the chance to play. I've been playing football.'"

DeFrancesco: "But sitting there at the PressBox and just looking at Josh – never once did he chime in on the game or a play or anything – he just kind of sat there and watched and didn't really say much."

Panelli: "I could just tell in his face, I wouldn't say he was aggravated, but it was getting to him a little bit. He knew they were just a few plays away from playing another week, from playing against the Chiefs."

Sorensen: "It really wasn't that weird until they started showing highlights of him playing. And then I'm looking at him and looking at his highlights on TV and then we're all kind of laughing, joking."

Panelli: "I think, determination wise, that unsettling feeling of knowing that we were in there watching in a town in the Central Valley that he's familiar with, and people are starting to get familiar with him and who he is, that was kind of a reminder about where he's at and where he's come from, but also where he's heading."

DeFrancesco: "I think the loss to Houston fueled him a ton. And not just the loss. The loss sucks, but the doubt that came with it. 'Is Josh the guy for Buffalo?' I think getting (quarterback Jake) Fromm in the next draft class kind of ignited that fire under him again and he acted like, 'I'm going to come out this season and show you guys that I am the quarterback for this franchise.'"

Panelli: "I almost saw like something clicked and he realized, 'What are some of the things we could have done different?' And those things were replaying in his head. He mentioned a few plays that could have gone differently, that would have changed the outcome of the game."

DeFrancesco: "Everything that came after that loss and what people were saying really fueled the fire to establish himself as the franchise quarterback in Buffalo. We all know that's where we'd prefer Josh to be. We love when he's down playing golf with us, hanging out, but we'd much rather have him go all the way to the Super Bowl."

Sorensen: "I hope he gets to play in the Super Bowl against (Tom) Brady. That was his guy growing up. I went to the (Bills' regular season) game a couple of years ago when they were playing the Patriots and Josh was hurt that game. He's always been a big Brady fan, so I know he wants to play Brady in the Super Bowl."

Panelli: "Cornhole, golf, football, video games, constantly talking (junk). That's what gets him to tick, is being competitive and knowing he belongs on that stage, too. And going into this year, he finally realized, 'This is where I belong. I can settle in.' And now we're watching him heading to the AFC championship game."

DeFrancesco: "It's due. He's due for all this. Everyone knows when you talk about Josh, he took the JUCO route, he had one DI offer at Wyoming. He's been putting in this work for a long time."

Panelli: "Later, at the end of the game, we're leaving. And I get up and turn around because we're facing the TV and our backs are to the rest of the restaurant, and there's about 15 people lined up at the bar and everybody's looking at us as we're walking out of there."

Sorensen: "And then Josh said something like, 'I don't think I'll be playing golf with you boys this time next year. I think I'll be playing football still.' And we're all kind of laughing and joking like, 'Oh, sure. We'll see about that. We'll be right here waiting for you.'" ∎

Watching the NFL playoffs at home after the Bills were eliminated the previous season gave Josh Allen the determination to lead Buffalo to the AFC Championship game following the 2020 season. (James P. McCoy/Buffalo News)

'WE WILL BE BACK'

Allen Reflects on Game That Got Away

By Jason Wolf | January 24, 2021

Josh Allen's dream matchup against Tom Brady in Super Bowl LV ended with a splash of cold water in Kansas City.

The Buffalo Bills quarterback's remarkable third pro season came to an unsatisfying close with a 38-24 loss to the defending Super Bowl champion Kansas City Chiefs in the AFC Championship Game Sunday night at Arrowhead Stadium. The loss dashed Buffalo's hopes of winning the first Super Bowl in franchise history and ended its deepest postseason run since 1994.

"It's going to fuel us," Allen said, echoing his comments after last year's wild-card playoff loss to the Houston Texans. "I've got no doubt in my mind that we will be back. This is a team that fought hard till the end, a team that loves each other. We're still young. We're only going to get better. That's one takeaway I've got from this. We're close. And the results weren't good tonight, but I'm super proud of how our team fought the entire season and how we bonded together."

It's worth remembering that the Jim Kelly-led Bills lost their first trip to the AFC title game in 1988, before advancing to four consecutive Super Bowls in the early 1990s. But that's of little solace today, as local sporting goods stores return unopened boxes of Bills Super Bowl merchandise.

The Chiefs will play the Buccaneers on Feb. 7 at Raymond James Stadium in Tampa, where the Bucs will become the first team in NFL history to play a Super Bowl on their home field.

Brady led No. 5-seeded Tampa Bay to a 31-26 victory over the top-seeded Green Bay Packers in the NFC title game, advancing to the 10th Super Bowl in his illustrious career.

The NFL will play all 267 scheduled games this season, despite the Covid-19 pandemic.

The Bills' season lasted until the penultimate contest.

"Sometimes the farther you go, the harder it is to lose," Bills coach Sean McDermott said. "It's a learning experience for us as an organization."

Allen completed 28 of 48 pass attempts for 287 yards, two touchdowns and an interception at the Kansas City 12-yard line, though much of that production came in garbage time. His 28 completions were second in franchise history for a playoff game behind Kelly's 31 against Dallas in the Super Bowl in 1994.

He nearly threw two more interceptions when the outcome was in doubt.

He couldn't convert in the red zone after leading long drives to the Chiefs' 2- and 8-yard lines, resulting in the Bills settling for field goals before halftime and in the third quarter.

And he left upset at himself after a skirmish broke out toward the end of the game when Allen was sacked and tossed the ball at the helmet of the Chiefs' Alex Okafor. Jon Feliciano and Dion Dawkins came to his defense, and multiple penalties were called.

Josh Allen throws a pass during the second quarter of the AFC Championship game. Allen completed 28 passes for 287 yards and two touchdowns in the loss. (James P. McCoy/Buffalo News)

"The way it ended doesn't sit right with me in how chippy and ticky tack it got" Allen said. "I'm disappointed in myself that I let my emotions get to me there. That's not how you're supposed to play the game of football."

Allen didn't receive much help. His receivers were largely shut down by the Kansas City defense, to the point where T.J. Yeldon had more receiving yards than Stefon Diggs for much of the game.

Cole Beasley led the Bills with seven catches for 88 yards. Diggs finished with six catches for 77 yards. John Brown was limited to two catches for 24 yards and Gabriel Davis was shut out on three targets.

Tight end Dawson Knox had six catches for 42 yards and a touchdown. Isaiah McKenzie caught the other touchdown from six yards out in the fourth quarter.

The Bills, as usual, received no support from the running game.

Allen led the team with 88 yards on seven carries. Devin Singletary offered a paltry 17 yards on six carries and two catches for nine yards, plus a drive-killing drop. Yeldon provided 15 yards on three carries and four catches for 41 yards.

The Bills raced to a 9-0 lead in the first quarter, when Tyler Bass kicked a 51-yard field goal and Chiefs wide receiver Mecole Hardman muffed a punt, which Buffalo running back Taiwan Jones recovered on the Kansas City 3-yard line. Moments later, Allen flipped a three-yard touchdown pass to Knox. But Bass missed the extra point, an omen for the offensive struggle to come.

Patrick Mahomes led the Chiefs to touchdowns on their next three possessions, racing to a 21-9 lead while the Bills' offense sputtered.

Buffalo trailed by two scores for the rest of the game.

"We try to tell him he doesn't have to put the whole organization on his shoulders," defensive end Jerry Hughes said about Allen. "He's got us to where we wanted to be, so for us on defense, we've got to help him out."

Allen responded by leading the Bills on an 11-play, 73-yard drive that stalled at the Kansas City 2-yard line. Bass kicked a 20-yard field goal to trim the deficit to 21-12 at halftime. He also booted a 27-yard field goal to cut it to 24-15 with about six minutes remaining in the third quarter.

But two touchdown catches by Travis Kelce, which sandwiched an Allen interception by Rashad Fenton at the Kansas City 12, ended any doubts about the outcome.

"You've got to put six on the board when you're facing Pat," Bills center Mitch Morse said.

Allen was a revelation this season, setting numerous single-season franchise records on the way to a 13-3 regular season mark, a franchise-record 501 points scored by the offense and the Bills' first AFC East championship since 1995.

He was a bona fide NFL MVP candidate and named the Most Improved Player in the league by the Pro Football Writers of America.

And he accomplished these feats despite the challenge of virtual offseason workouts, no preseason and little time to become acquainted with Diggs, the superstar wide receiver who led the NFL in catches and receiving yards after being acquired in a trade from the Minnesota Vikings on March 16, just days after Covid-19 turned our world on its head.

And he did it despite personal heartache.

Allen produced one of the finest games of his career a day after his grandmother passed away in November, when he completed more than 80% of his passes for a career-high-tying 415 yards and three touchdowns in a 44-34 victory against Seattle.

Allen didn't publicize his family's loss.

McDermott first mentioned it after the game, which led to Bills fans donating more than a million dollars in Patricia Allen's memory to Oishei Children's Hospital.

Allen, likewise, didn't publicize that his father, Joel, had been admitted to a hospital this month while fighting Covid-19 and pneumonia.

He nevertheless guided the Bills to eight consecutive victories and the AFC title game.

Allen's dad, who is recovering, remained home and did not attend any of the Bills' playoff games. His mother, LaVonne, and other family and friends traveled to Kansas City.

Josh Allen is sacked by Kansas City Chiefs defensive end Tanoh Kpassagnon during the fourth quarter of the AFC Championship game. Allen was sacked four times in the loss. (James P. McCoy/Buffalo News)

"It was a tough adjustment this year with all the coronavirus and the testing and separating and not being able to go over teammates' houses, and just the sacrifice that it took this year," Allen said. "I'm super proud of what we did this year."

An article about Allen's Northern California roots that published on Saturday in the Los Angeles Times was accompanied by an image of framed photos hanging on a wall in the Allen family ranch in Firebaugh, Calif.

In one, the Bills' quarterback is seen jumping over Vikings linebacker Anthony Barr, a 6-foot-5, 255-pound four-time Pro Bowler, during the Bills' stunning 27-6 upset victory in 2018, the first NFL victory of Allen's career.

In another photo, Allen is seen meeting Brady on the field after a game in New England.

"He's always been a big Brady fan," one of Allen's longtime friends told The News last week, "so I know he wants to play Brady in the Super Bowl."

Brady has a 6-3 record in nine Super Bowl appearances with the Patriots.

Allen is winless in three games against the Brady, never beating New England until sweeping the AFC East this season. Allen is likewise winless in two games against Mahomes.

"At the end of the day, this is our measuring stick," McDermott said. "If you lose in the AFC Championship Game, that's the team we've got to beat."

There's always next season. ∎

THE FUTURE LOOKS BRIGHT

Here's Where Allen Stands in Under-25 History

By Mark Gaughan | May 21, 2021

Josh Allen turns 25 years old today.

Happy birthday, Josh, you've already accomplished a lot in three NFL seasons.

Actually, the Buffalo quarterback has done more than even the most loyal fan clad in a No. 17 Bills jersey might realize.

Allen has produced 92 touchdowns – 67 passing and 25 rushing. That's tied for third among quarterbacks in NFL history before the age of 25. The only players who produced more before turning 25 were Dan Marino, who had 104, and Jameis Winston, who had 97. Cam Newton also had 92 by 25 – but in five more starts than Allen.

Allen also ranks tied for fifth in most regular-season wins by a starting quarterback by age 25. He's 28-15 overall ... 30-17 if you count the postseason. Bernie Kosar also had 28 regular-season wins by 25. The only quarterbacks with more? Marino at 34, Drew Bledsoe 32, Lamar Jackson 30 and Ben Roethlisberger 29. Baltimore's Jackson, 24, still has one more full season to play before he turns 25.

The future undeniably looks bright for Allen.

"Josh is a cornerstone to our foundation and our organization," coach Sean McDermott said after the conclusion of the 2020 season.

"He's an extremely driven young man with a bright future," McDermott said. "There are very few parts of his game that aren't developed after his third season, that you say, 'Well, he really struggles in this area.' I think it's a small conversation of things that he needs to evolve in. He would tell you probably the same in those areas. I've seen him do much of what it takes to win and win at a high level. I think he answered quite a few of the questions that were out there about him, maybe from outside this building, specifically about his play."

Allen also ranks 11th in yards among QBs before age 25, 10th in attempts and 12th in TD passes.

He's in mostly outstanding company among the under-25 leaders. Marino, of course, is a Hall of Famer. Hall of Famer Peyton Manning is fifth in TDs produced. Houston's Deshaun Watson is sixth, Jackson seventh, the Rams' Matthew Stafford eighth and Kansas City's Patrick Mahomes is tied for ninth.

Almost all the players among the under-25 QB leaders are from the past two decades, because underclassmen weren't allowed to enter the NFL draft until 1990. And quarterbacks used to be eased into starting roles over their first couple of seasons. That practice mostly has disappeared the past decade or so.

There is some cautionary company, however – players who weren't able to maintain early success in their careers.

One is Winston, the former first overall pick of Tampa Bay who this year will battle for the starting job in New Orleans. They also include ex-Buc Josh Freeman, who made the second-most starts by age 25, and Blake Bortles, who is eighth in passing yards at 11,241.

However, there were clear warning signs that they weren't headed for elite quarterbacking futures.

In his first three seasons, Josh Allen produced 92 touchdowns — 67 passing and 25 rushing. Only Dan Marino and Jameis Winston produced more touchdowns before turning 25. (Harry Scull Jr./Buffalo News)

Besides his prolific yards and TD totals, Winston also has the second-most losses (33) and the eighth-most interceptions (58) of any under-25 QB. Winston, now 27, is the most interception-prone active QB in the league. It was a similar story for ex-Buc Freeman, who has the third-most losses (32) and the sixth-most interceptions (63). Freeman, in fact, was out of the NFL by age 28. Bortles has the most losses (34) of any QB by age 25 and the most pick-sixes (11). Bortles lost his job with Jacksonville after his age-26 season and recently was signed by Green Bay to compete for a backup spot in training camp.

Obviously, no one can guarantee the trajectory of any player's career. But none of those kinds of warning signs exists with Allen, who has thrown fewer than half the interceptions of Winston and Freeman and has fewer than half the losses Bortles had.

And none of those QBs – who soon lost their starting jobs – ever produced a season similar to the one Allen had in 2020, when he produced 45 TDs with 10 interceptions and finished second in most valuable player voting.

Allen was 22 years and 3 months old when he made his first NFL start, on Sept. 16, 2018, against the Los Angeles Chargers.

That early ascension to the starting job has helped him put up big numbers compared with his peers. Allen ranks 11th in starts before age 25 with 43.

Kansas City's Mahomes was eight days shy of his 23rd birthday when he took over the Chiefs' QB job at the start of the 2018 season. Mahomes' pre-25 numbers are a little shy of Allen's because Mahomes made only 32 starts before age 25, 11 less than Allen did.

If you want to compare the same number of starts, Mahomes far exceeded Allen through 43 starts, posting a 35-8 record with 13,227 yards and 113 total touchdowns.

Mahomes was 24 years and 118 days old when he capped the 2019 season by winning the Super Bowl MVP award. He's the youngest player to win it.

Allen is eight months younger than Mahomes. He's never catching him in that department.

But as Allen turns 25, Bills fans can dream about all the lofty numbers still to come for their No. 17.

"We're excited at what we have in No. 17 and where that's going and really appreciative of how hard he's worked since we selected him back in 2018," General Manager Brandon Beane said. "Just looking forward to what he's gonna do this offseason and what he's gonna look like in 2021." ■

Josh Allen does a postgame interview after the Bills' victory over the Indianapolis Colts on Jan. 9, 2021 — the first Bills playoff win since 1995. (Harry Scull Jr./Buffalo News)